SCHOLASTIC

AF207654

GRADES 2–3

Sequencing Practice Mini-Books

By Kathleen M. Hollenbeck

New York · Toronto · London · Auckland · Sydney
Mexico City · New Delhi · Hong Kong · Buenos Aires

Teaching *Resources*

Scholastic Inc. grants teachers permission to photocopy the reproducible pages from this book for classroom use. No other part of this publication may be reproduced in whole or in part, or stored in a retrieval system, or transmitted in any form or by any means, electronic, mechanical, photocopying, recording, or otherwise, without written permission of the publisher. For information regarding permission, write to Scholastic Inc., 557 Broadway, New York, NY 10012.

Edited by Immacula A. Rhodes
Cover design by Jason Robinson
Cover illustrations by Anne Kennedy
Interior design by Sydney Wright
Interior illustrations by Anne Kennedy and Mike Moran

ISBN-13: 978-0-545-24803-7
ISBN-10: 0-545-24803-5

Copyright © 2010 by Kathleen M. Hollenbeck
Illustrations © 2010 by Scholastic Inc.
Published by Scholastic Inc.
All rights reserved.
Printed in the U.S.A.

2 3 4 5 6 7 8 9 10   40   17 16 15 14 13 12 11 10

Contents

Introduction 4

How to Make the Mini-Books 5

Extension Activities 7

Connections to the Language Arts Standards 8

Fall Mini-Books

School Days Long Ago 9

Make a Friendly Pumpkin 13

Fire Safety Field Trip 17

Hurrah for Thanksgiving! 23

Winter Mini-Books

America's First Woman Doctor 27

How to Build a Snow Person 31

Crocodile Smile 35

Gus Groundhog's Surprise 40

Spring Mini-Books

Life on the Space Station 44

Nicole Makes the Team 48

Growing Up in a Pond 52

The Magic Bar of Soap 58

Summer Mini-Books

Growing Sunflowers 62

Happy Birthday, America! 66

Make Your Own Smoothie 72

Answer Key 76

Introduction

Welcome to *Sequencing Practice Mini-Books: Grades 2–3!* The 15 mini-books in this resource are designed to improve students' reading comprehension by focusing on a key skill: sequencing. In developing sequencing skills, students apply critical thinking to assess story events, understand what is happening, predict what comes next, and arrange events in a logical order from beginning to end. These mini-books also help deepen students' awareness of story structure.

Organized by season, these easy-to-make mini-books feature fiction and nonfiction topics including fire safety, dental hygiene, living on the space station, the development of a frog, plant growth, and more. The variety of formats challenges students to examine picture and/or text clues—including important time-order vocabulary, such as *first, next, then, after, last,* and *finally*—to sequence the pages for assembly. The mini-books in each group increase in difficulty to provide maximum flexibility, allowing you to meet the needs of students at different ability levels as well as to create a progression of sequencing activities that reflect their growing comprehension skills. You can use the mini-books for whole-class or partner activities or in small groups. The books also work well as learning-center or take-home activities.

Finally, and perhaps most important, the mini-books are designed to reinforce the idea that reading is both useful and fun. As students assemble the mini-books, they'll come to recognize the need for honoring sequence, especially when performing a task or ordering the steps to follow when constructing a project such as a snow person. In the process, students strengthen important reading skills, including comprehension, using context clues, making predictions, and more.

Why Sequencing Is Important

Recognizing sequence plays an important role in children's reading comprehension. "Readers can discover a sequence in connected illustrations: chronological order, cycles of action from home to an adventure and back home, flashbacks, embedded stories. Attention to the illustrations can support understanding of text structure (thinking about the text)" (Fountas & Pinnell, 2006). Whether in pictures or text, early exposure to sequencing opens the gateway to thinking critically, helping children apply prior knowledge to understand unfamiliar texts, storylines, and procedures.

As children progress from pre-reading to becoming proficient readers, sequencing stories fosters the development of other skills within Bloom's Taxonomy, helping children to predict, summarize, explain, and discuss story events. Understanding how events play out—in stories and real life—aids readers in anticipating what comes next and in recognizing what is expected, reasonable, and logical. When this occurs, comprehension deepens.

To progress in reading, readers must also understand the most basic nature of the story itself. "*Knowledge of narrative structure* involves understanding the nature of stories and how they are constructed. Knowledge of the structure of stories is important because most of the material used to teach reading to young children is written in narrative form. Children are likely to understand material presented in a form with which they are familiar" (Strickland, 1998). Understanding sequence helps children better understand the structure of a story and aids them in recalling and recounting important events in an organized, logical way.

Resources

Fountas, Irene C. and Gay Su Pinnell, 2006. *Teaching for comprehending and fluency: Thinking, talking, and writing about reading, K–8.* Portsmouth, NH: Heinemann.

Strickland, Dorothy S., 1998. *Teaching phonics today: A primer for educators.* Newark, DE: International Reading Association.

Sequencing Practice Mini-Books, Grades 2–3 © 2010 by Kathleen M. Hollenbeck, Scholastic Teaching Resources

How to Make the Mini-Books

Copy the reproducible patterns for each mini-book, including text boxes where applicable. Distribute the patterns to students and have them assemble their mini-books according to the type of mini-book they'll be constructing (see below). After they correctly order and number the pages, have students stack and staple the pages together behind the cover. (If needed, use the Answer Key on pages 76–80 to check the page sequence before binding the mini-book.)

Illustrations and Text

Students will use picture and text clues to sequence the pages of these mini-books.

1. After distributing the pages, point out that they have pictures and text on them.

2. Tell students to look for clues in the illustrations and text that will help them sequence the pages.

3. After students correctly order the pages, have them fill in the page numbers.

School Days Long Ago
   (page 9)
America's First Woman
   Doctor (page 27)
Life on the Space Station
   (page 44)
The Magic Bar of Soap
   (page 58)
Growing Sunflowers
   (page 62)

Before You Start

The mini-book pages are sequenced in the correct order in this resource. To distribute the pages in random order, copy a class supply of the mini-book pages and use a paper cutter to cut the pages apart. You can then stack the pages for each mini-book in random order before distributing them to students.

Text Only

Students use text clues to sequence these mini-books and then add their own illustrations to complete them.

1. After distributing the pages, point out that they contain text, but no pictures.

2. Have students read each page, looking for clues in the text to help them sequence the pages. Offer guidance as needed.

3. After students correctly order the pages, have them draw a picture to match the text on each page and then fill in the page number. Also, have them illustrate the cover. Before they do, talk about how the illustration and title on a book's cover usually relate to the main idea of the story and help readers know what the book is about.

Make a Friendly Pumpkin
    (page 13)
Hurrah for Thanksgiving!
    (page 23)
How to Build a Snow
    Person (page 31)
Gus Groundhog's Surprise
    (page 40)
Nicole Makes the Team
    (page 48)
Make Your Own Smoothie
    (page 72)

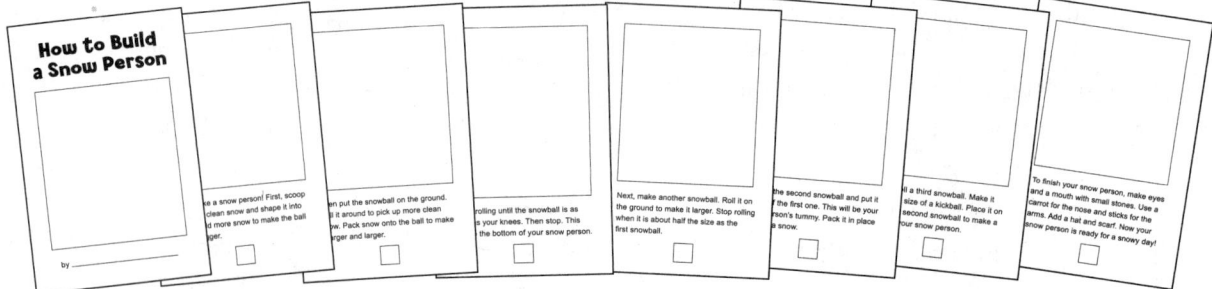

Illustrations Only

Students pair text boxes to illustrations and then sequence the pages to complete these mini-books.

1. After distributing the pages, have students cut out the seven text boxes.

2. Point out that each page of the book has a picture as well as an empty box under the picture. Explain that students will read the text boxes and then use picture clues to match each text box to its corresponding picture. Once they've matched the correct text to each page, have students glue the text boxes to the pages.

3. Instruct students to use picture and text clues to put the pages in order. After they correctly order the pages, have them fill in the page numbers.

Fire Safety Field Trip
    (page 17)
Crocodile Smile
    (page 35)
Growing Up in a Pond
    (page 52)
Happy Birthday, America!
    (page 66)

Extension Activities

Use these additional ideas to help reinforce sequencing skills.

Circle Key Words: To aid in sequencing the mini-book pages, ask students to find and circle vocabulary that suggests time order, such as *first, next, after, later, last,* and *finally*. Then encourage students to use the words as guides to sequence their pages.

Mix It Up: Bind the mini-book pages with brass fasteners instead of staples. Then ask students to disassemble their books, mix up the pages, and sequence them again. If possible, change the stories so that events happen in a different order. Does the story still make sense? How might restructuring the events change the outcome of the story?

What's Next?: Put students at the other end of the sequencing cycle. Ask them to write their own sequence of steps for common activities such as washing hands, making a bed, feeding a pet, or making a sandwich. Have them write each step on a separate index card and then number the back of the cards in sequential order. Later, pair up students and have the partners sequence each other's set of cards.

Does It Really Matter?: Does it matter whether students rinse their hands before or after washing them with soap? Does it matter which items of clothing they put on before others? Talk about why following a logical sequence is important in some situations and not in others. Then invite students to give examples of events or situations in which order does and does not matter. (Examples in which order does not matter might include the sequence in which foods are eaten during a meal or choosing which homework to tackle first.) Record their examples on a two-column chart labeled "Order Matters" and "Order Does Not Matter." As students share, invite them to explain why the order does or does not matter.

Add to the Stories: Challenge students to think beyond the events in the story-oriented mini-books. What might have happened before the story started? What might have happened after the ending? Is there a fitting event they might be able to insert into the middle of the story? What sequencing clues might they include to tell where in the story the new event belongs? For example, the words "Years later, when I am a teacher . . ." might be appropriate linking words for an epilogue to "School Days Long Ago" (page 9).

Fortunately, Unfortunately . . . : Provide students with eight half-sheets of plain white paper. Then have them create their own mini-books based on the popular "Fortunately, Unfortunately" storytelling technique. For example, a student's story might begin, "Fortunately, I set my alarm before I went to sleep last night." On the next page, the student might follow up with "Unfortunately, I didn't hear the alarm go off." The text on the third page might be "Fortunately, my little brother woke me up." The student continues the story, alternating the fortunate and unfortunate cause-effect events to complete the mini-book. When completed, ask students to share their books, inviting classmates to put the pages in order.

Let the Stories Be Your Guide: Use the mini-book topics as springboards for students to create their own sequencing mini-books. For example, after working with "America's First Woman Doctor" (page 27), ask students to research other historical figures. Have them use the information they gather to write and illustrate a mini-book story. Encourage them to use sequencing signal words such as *first, next, then, before, after, last,* and *finally* in their text. When finished, have students stack and staple the pages behind a cover. If desired, ask them to omit the page numbers. Then punch holes in the pages and bind them with a metal ring. Later, have students take apart their mini-books, mix up the pages, and give them to a partner to sequence.

Connections to the Language Arts Standards

Mid-continent Research for Education and Learning (McREL), a nationally recognized nonprofit organization, has compiled and evaluated national and state standards—and proposed what teachers should provide for their Grades 2–3 students to grow proficient in reading. The activities in this book support the following standards:

Uses the general skills and strategies of the reading process including:
- Uses mental images and meaning clues based on pictures and print to aid in comprehension of text
- Makes, confirms, and revises simple predictions about what will be found in text
- Uses phonetic and structural analysis techniques, syntactic structure, and semantic context to decode unknown words
- Understands level-appropriate reading vocabulary
- Uses self-correction strategies

Uses reading skills and strategies to understand and interpret a variety of literary texts including:
- Understands a variety of literary passages and texts
- Understands the basic concept of plot

Uses reading skills and strategies to understand and interpret a variety of informational texts including:
- Understands a variety of informational texts
- Understands the main idea and supporting details of simple expository information
- Summarizes and paraphrases information in texts
- Relates new information to prior knowledge and experience
- Understands structural patterns or organization of informational texts

Source: Kendall, J. S., & Marzano, R. J. (2004). *Content knowledge: A compendium of standards and benchmarks for K–12 education.* Aurora, CO: Mid-continent Research for Education and Learning. Online database: **http://www.mcrel.org/standards-benchmarks/**

Sequencing Practice Mini-Books, Grades 2–3 © 2010 by Kathleen M. Hollenbeck, Scholastic Teaching Resources

School Days
Long Ago

by _____

Today is the first day of school!
We go to school all winter and summer.
In the spring and fall, we stay home to
work on the farm. My brother and I walk
an hour to get to school.

When we reach the school, we go inside. Our school has only one room. Boys and girls of all ages are in the same class.

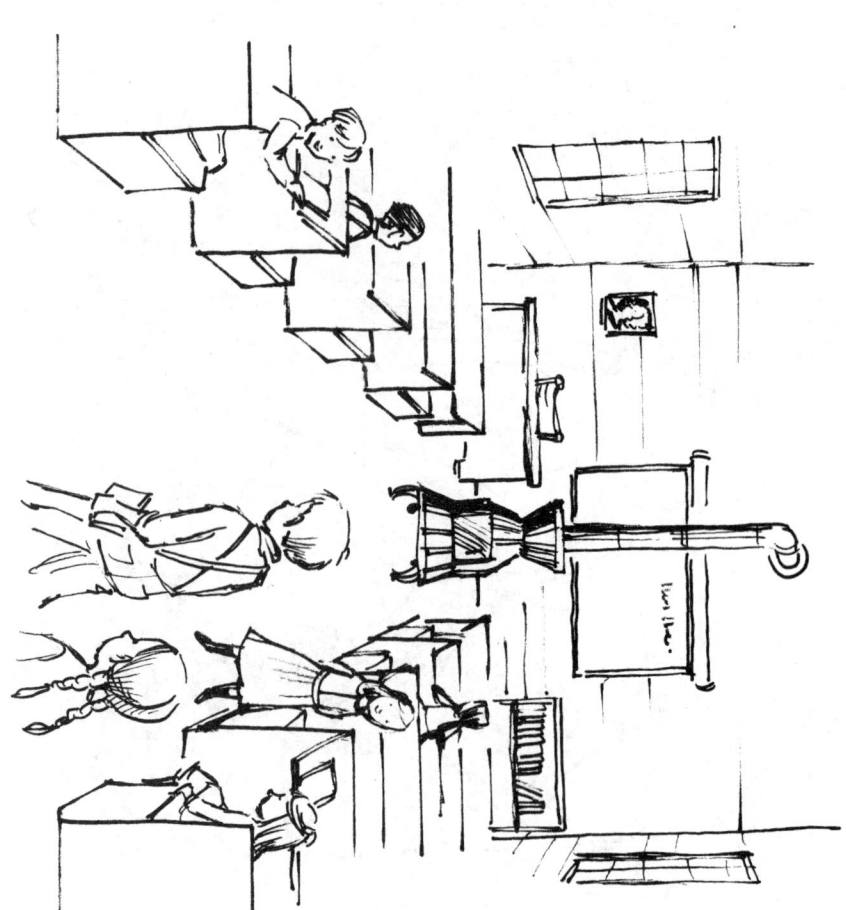

Right away, we meet our teacher, Miss Marks. Then we take our seats. Soon, Miss Marks speaks to the whole class. She tells us what to read in our books.

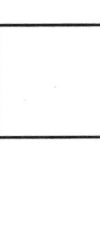

After reading, we practice writing words on small chalkboards called slates. We also work on our math facts. I help the younger children learn their ABC's until lunchtime.

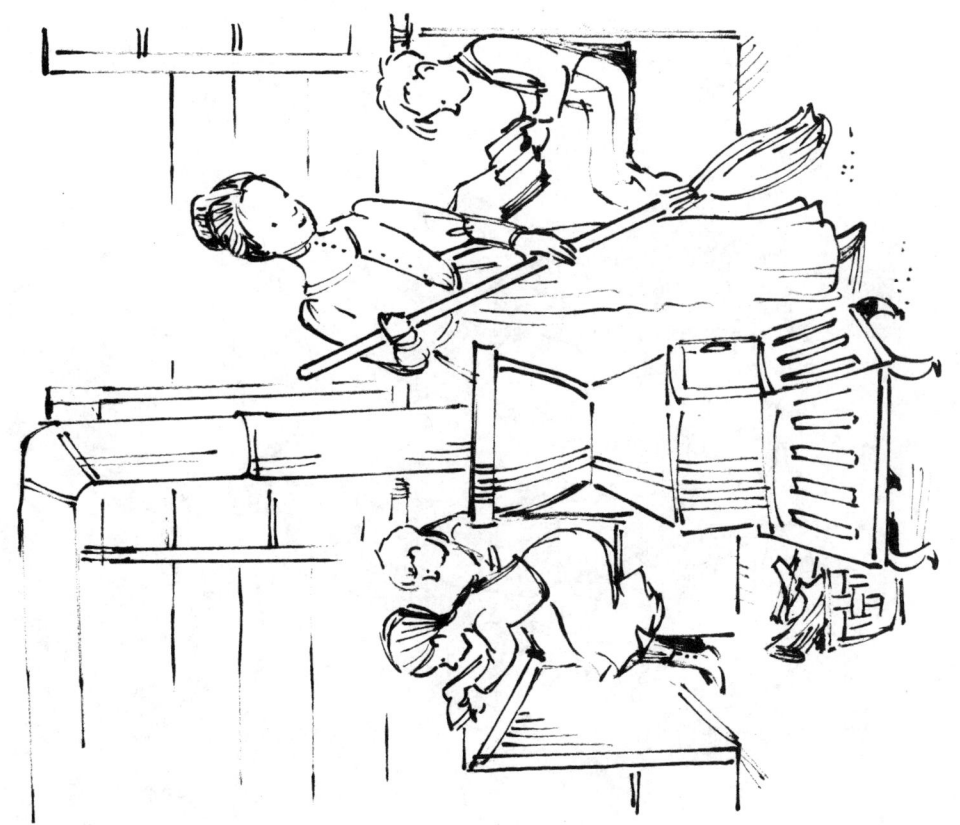

While we read on our own, Miss Marks sweeps the floor. She also puts logs in the woodstove. Miss Marks has many jobs during the school day.

Some children walk home for lunch.
My brother and I bring our lunch in a pail.
We eat under a tree and then play tag.
When Miss Marks rings the bell, we
go back inside for more lessons.

At last, the school day ends. Snow
begins to fall as we walk home. I don't
mind, though. I think about my first day
at school. I'm excited about all the new
things I'll learn this winter!

Make a Friendly Pumpkin

by _____

How can you turn a plain pumpkin into a friendly face? Carve it!

First, you need to get a pumpkin.

Next, find a permanent marker, a spoon, and a plastic carving knife. You'll also need a sturdy nail.

When you have everything you need, you're ready to get started. To begin, ask a grown-up to cut out the top of the pumpkin.

After you clean out the pumpkin, use the marker to draw a friendly face on it. Draw large shapes for the eyes, nose, and mouth. Keep the shapes simple so they will be easy to cut out.

Lift the top off the pumpkin. Then scoop out the seeds and pulp inside the pumpkin. Use the spoon to do this.

Does the face look the way you want it?
If so, poke holes along the lines of your
shapes. Use the nail to make the holes.
Be sure the holes go all the way through
the pumpkin shell.

☐

Finally, get a grown-up to help you
cut out the face. Use the plastic
carving knife to cut from one hole to
the next. Then push out the pieces.
Now you have a friendly pumpkin!

☐

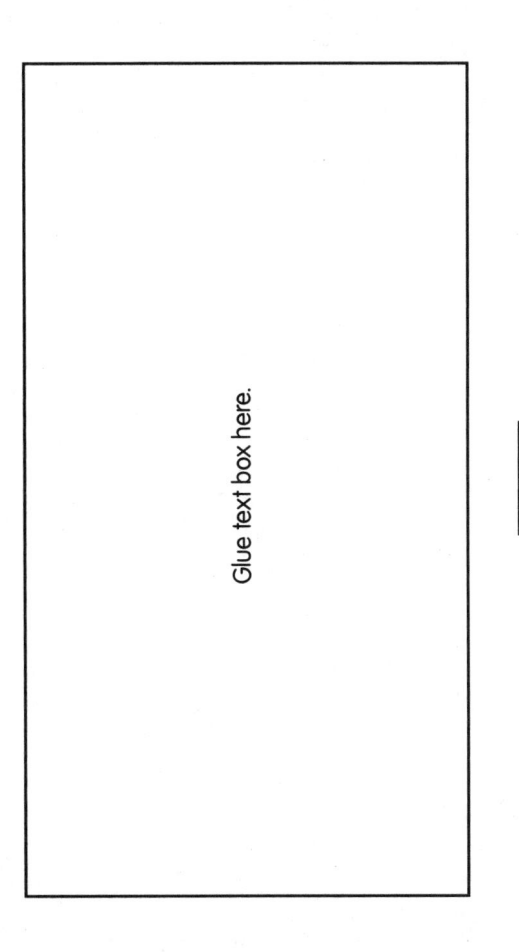

Glue text box here.

Fire Safety
Field Trip

by _____

Glue text box here.

Glue text box here.

Glue text box here.

Glue text box here.

Glue text box here.

Glue text box here.

Fire Safety Field Trip

Text Boxes

"Right! A smoke detector!" said Daniel.
"Your home needs one on every level.
It can warn your family of a fire.
Test it every month. Change the
batteries twice a year."

"Time for the second riddle," said Daniel.
"These small sticks look harmless
but can start a mighty fire.
Children, do not touch them.
Grown-ups, place them higher."
"Matches!" said Ben.

One morning, Mr. Bell's class visited
a fire station. A firefighter greeted the
children. "My name is Daniel," he said.
"We're going to solve some fire safety
riddles today!"

"Let's try an easy riddle first," Daniel
said with a grin.
"This is round and hangs on the wall.
When it goes off, it has a shrill call."
"A smoke detector!" guessed Jenna.

**Fire Safety
Field Trip**
Text Boxes

"Ready for the last riddle?"
asked Daniel.
"If there's smoke or fire,
this plan helps you know
how to get out quickly
and the safest place to go."

"A fire escape plan!" said Lou. "It shows
how to get out of a building safely."
"Great job with the riddles!" said Daniel.
"Now, let's tour the fire station!"

"Now for the third riddle," said Daniel.
"If your clothes catch fire,
there are three things you should do.
These will stop the flames and
keep the fire from harming you."
"Stop, drop, and roll!" said Kayla.

It's early in the morning on Thanksgiving Day. I get out of bed and get dressed. I can smell the turkey cooking downstairs. Suddenly, I hear a loud laugh. My favorite uncle is here!

Hurrah for Thanksgiving!

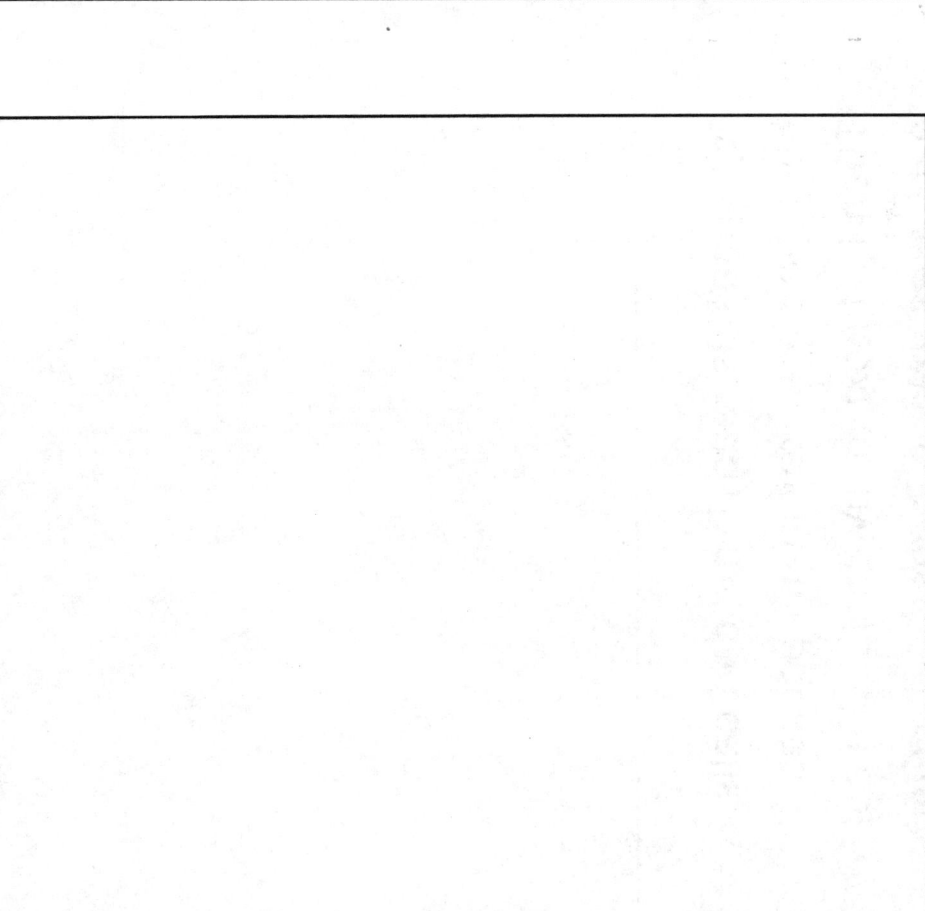

by _____

I race downstairs and hug my uncle.
He holds up a small toy turkey and
squeezes its tummy. A loud "Gobble!"
fills the air.

"Breakfast is ready!" my dad calls.
I put the toy turkey in my pocket.
Then I sit next to my uncle. We eat
pancakes, bacon, eggs, and muffins.

At noon, the doorbell rings. It's my grandparents, aunt, and cousins! We all talk and laugh together for a while. Then we gather at the table and give thanks for dinner. We pass around plates of turkey, stuffing, and squash.

As soon as we finish breakfast, the clock chimes nine o'clock. My uncle and I race into the den and turn on the TV. We draw pictures and talk as we watch the holiday parade.

After dinner, the grown-ups watch football on TV. The rest of us play games. Before long, we take a break to eat pie, cookies, and cake until we are full.

Everyone leaves when it begins to get dark. At nine o'clock, I climb into bed. I feel thankful for my family and the day we shared. Hurrah for Thanksgiving! It's the best holiday ever!

Elizabeth Blackwell wanted to be a doctor. She needed to go to school to become one. At that time, only men were doctors. Most schools would not let a woman in.

America's First Woman Doctor

by _____

After many tries, Elizabeth found a school that would let her study there. People made fun of Elizabeth. They did not think women could be doctors.

In school, Elizabeth studied hard. She did well on her tests. She even finished at the top of her class! Elizabeth was the very first woman in America to become a doctor.

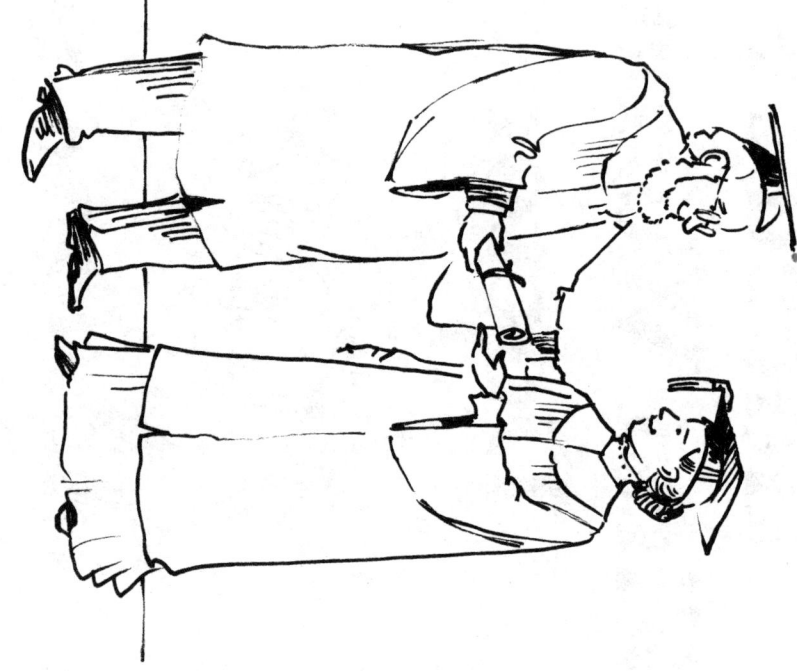

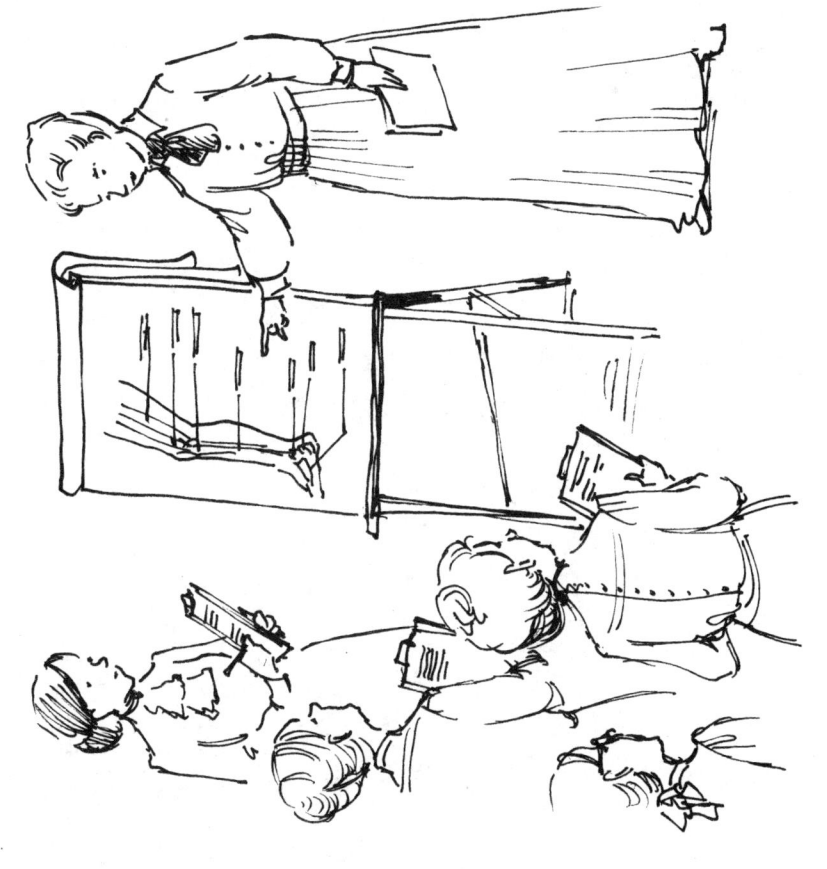

Dr. Blackwell worked from her house for years. Then she opened a hospital for women and children. She also trained others to become nurses.

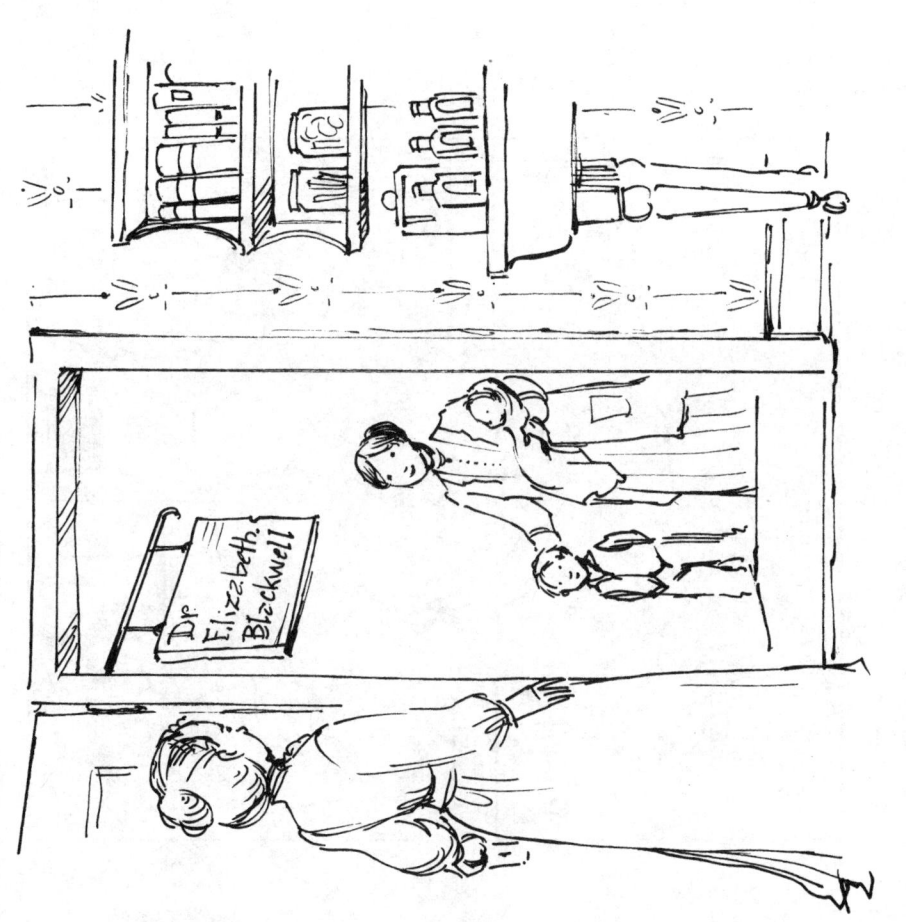

After graduating, Dr. Elizabeth Blackwell went to other countries to study and work. When she came back to America, no hospital would hire her. But Elizabeth had an idea! She bought a house and used it as a doctor's office!

Training nurses gave Dr. Blackwell another idea. She could start a school of her own! Dr. Blackwell began a medical college. Her college was for women who wanted to become doctors.

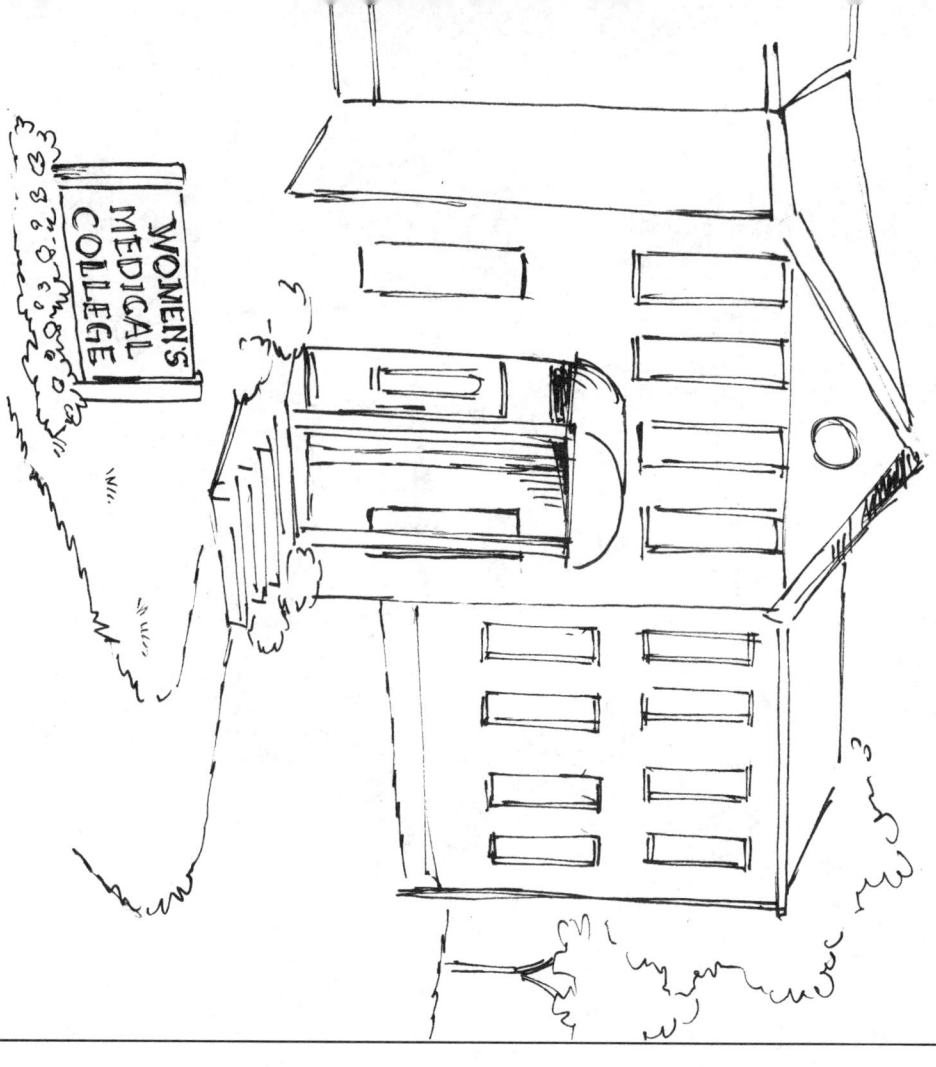

All of her life, Dr. Elizabeth Blackwell helped and served others. She worked hard and led the way for other women to become doctors. Dr. Blackwell made life better for women in America and all over the world.

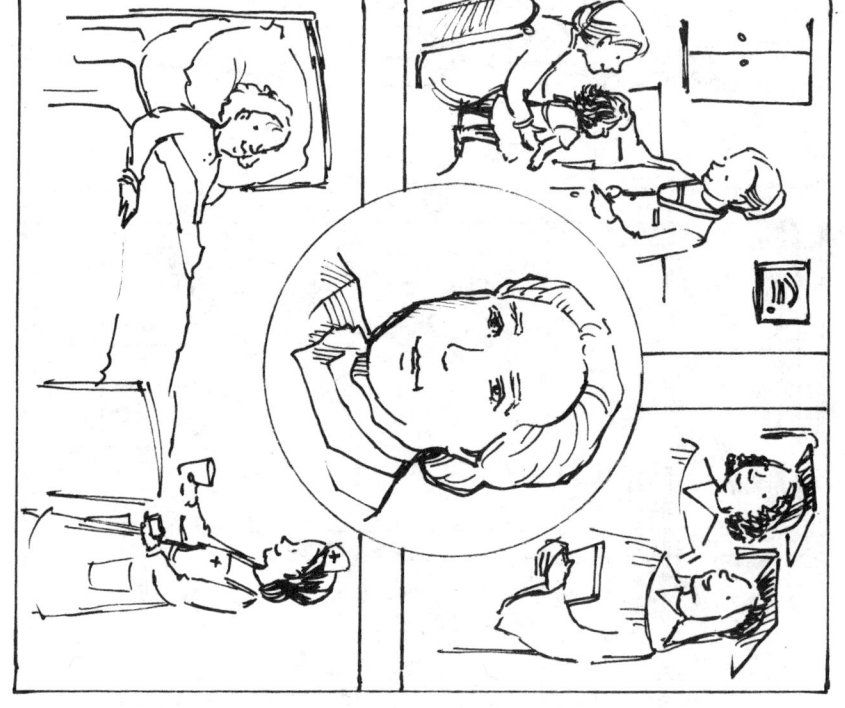

How to Build a Snow Person

by _____

Let's make a snow person! First, scoop up some clean snow and shape it into a ball. Add more snow to make the ball a little bigger.

Then put the snowball on the ground. Roll it around to pick up more clean snow. Pack snow onto the ball to make it larger and larger.

Keep rolling until the snowball is as high as your knees. Then stop. This will be the bottom of your snow person.

Pick up the second snowball and put it on top of the first one. This will be your snow person's tummy. Pack it in place with extra snow.

Next, make another snowball. Roll it on the ground to make it larger. Stop rolling when it is about half the size as the first snowball.

Finally, roll a third snowball. Make it about the size of a kickball. Place it on top of the second snowball to make a head for your snow person.

To finish your snow person, make eyes and a mouth with small stones. Use a carrot for the nose and sticks for the arms. Add a hat and scarf. Now your snow person is ready for a snowy day!

Glue text box here.

Crocodile Smile

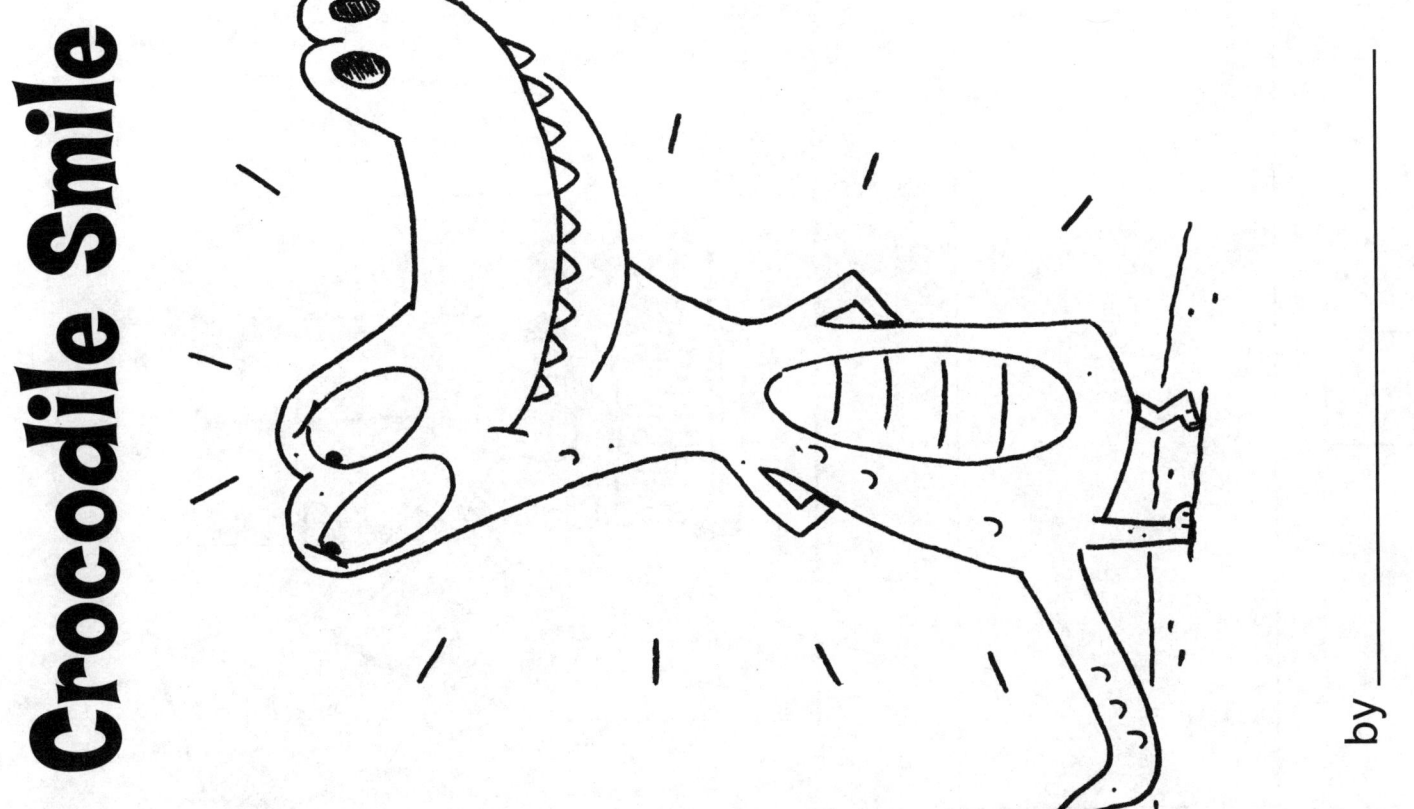

by _____

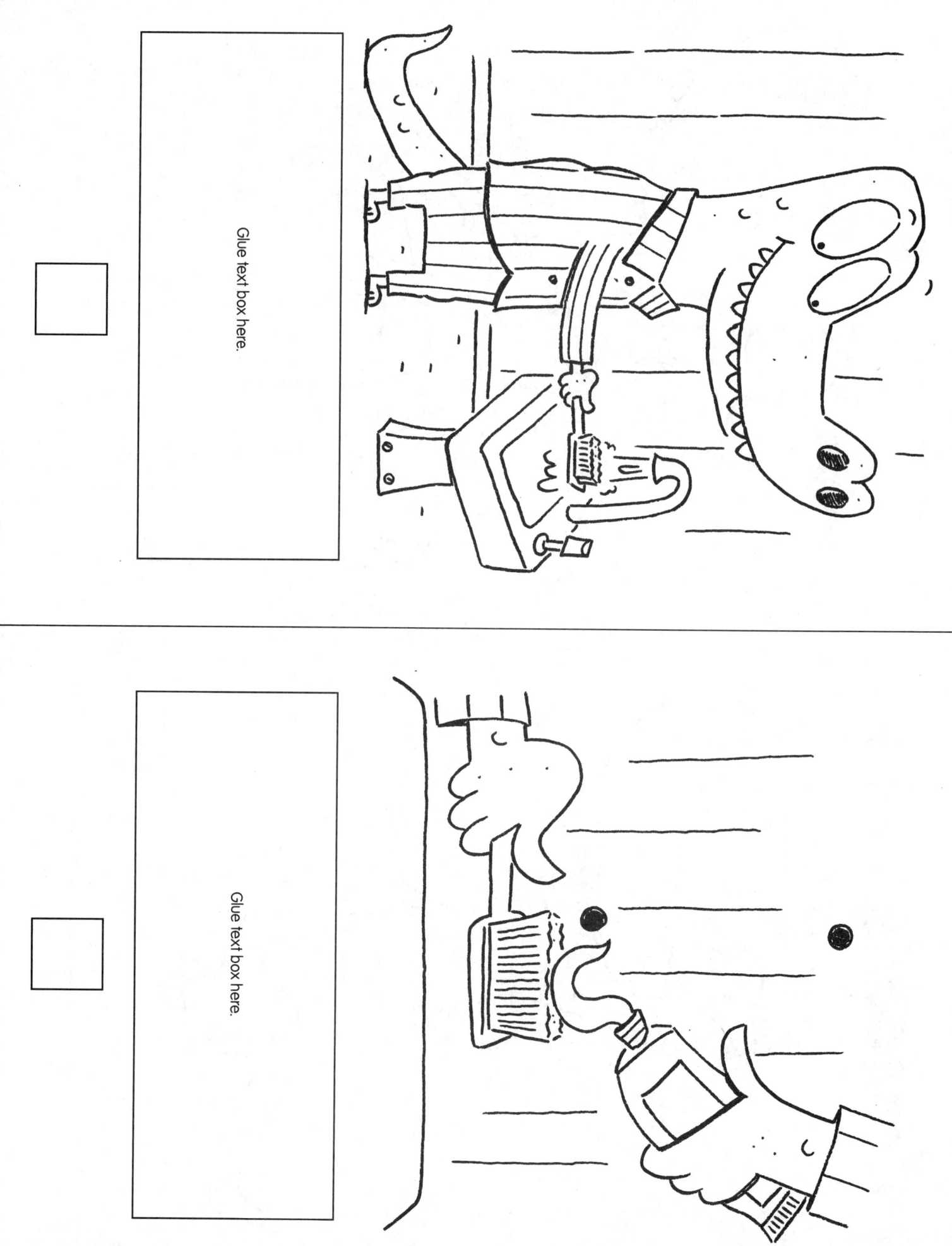

Glue text box here.

Glue text box here.

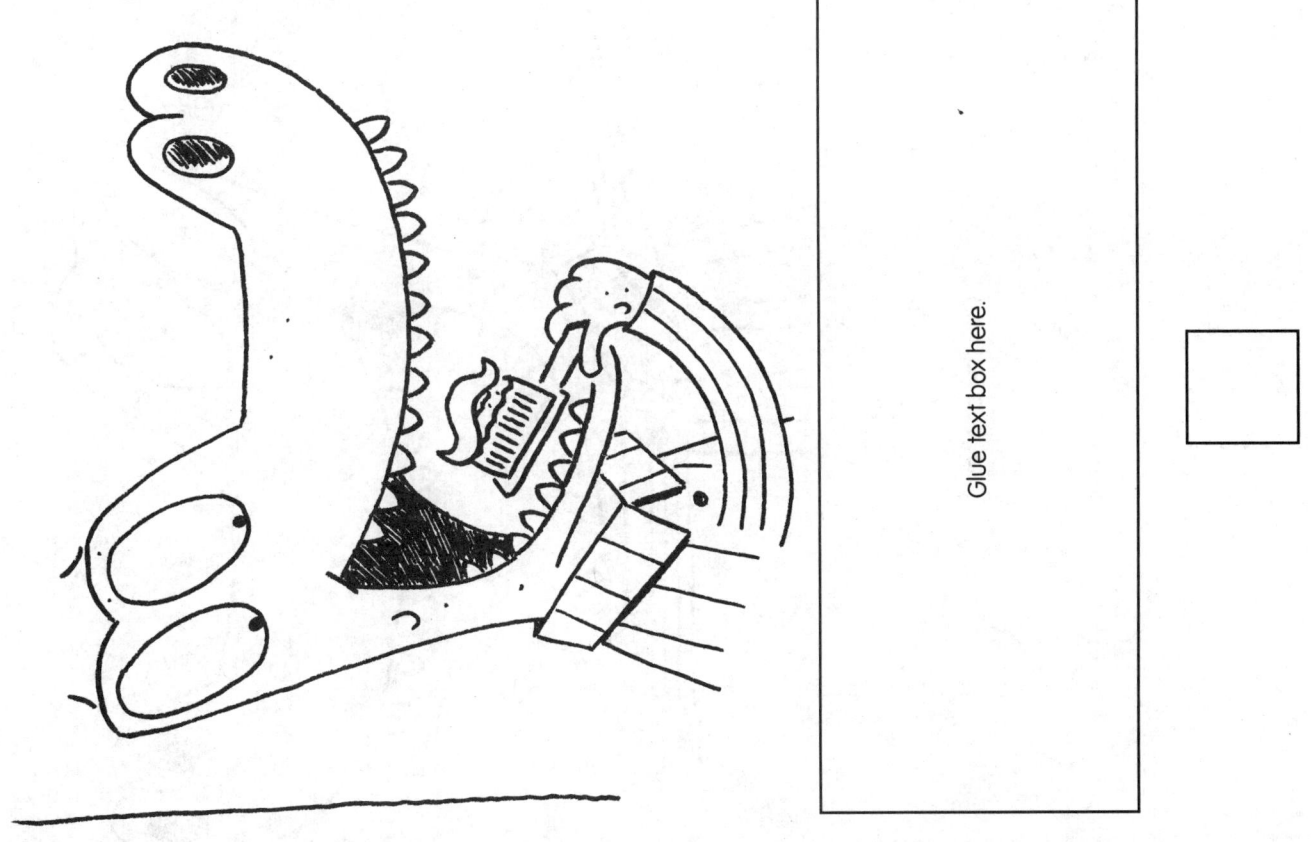

Glue text box here.

Glue text box here.

Glue text box here.

Glue text box here.

I open wide and start to brush.
I brush in circles, round and round.
I sweep the food and germs away.
My toothbrush makes a scrubbing sound.

I brush and brush, bottom and top.
I brush each tooth in front and back.
I brush in every spot I think
might be a hiding place for plaque.

I am a great big crocodile.
My teeth are pointed, sharp, and white.
I brush them every single day,
and then I brush again at night.

To start, I turn the water on
and hold my toothbrush underneath.
I like to get it nice and wet
so it will slide across my teeth.

Once this is done, I look around
until I find my own toothpaste.
I squeeze a little on my brush.
I really like the minty taste.

Crocodile Smile
Text Boxes

When I am done, my mouth is full.
I spit the foam into the sink.
I turn the water on again
to rinse my brush and get a drink.

I've brushed my teeth and now I know
I've taken good care of my smile.
My teeth feel clean. My job is done.
I am a happy crocodile.

Gus Groundhog's Surprise

by _____

Snow fell early on the morning of February 2nd. Gus Groundhog slept soundly, snug in his burrow under the ground.

"It's Groundhog Day!" he said.

"My friends must be waiting for me."

Gus hurried through his burrow.

He thought about the crowd that

would greet him. How they would

cheer when they saw him!

Suddenly, Gus awoke from his winter

nap. He stretched and yawned. Then he

checked the date on the calendar.

When Gus reached the opening of his burrow, he poked his head out of the hole. But no one was there. "How can this be?" asked Gus. "They've never missed my big day before!"

Gus crawled out and looked around. No one was in sight. He looked sadly at the ground. Even his shadow didn't show up to greet him.

"Happy Groundhog Day!" said his friends. Gus smiled and said, "I knew you would come! But my shadow didn't show up. Do you know what that means?"

"Hurray!" they all cheered. "Spring will be early this year!"

After a while, Gus turned to go back into his burrow. Then he saw something move behind some trees. Suddenly a big crowd appeared and called out "Surprise!" His friends had come after all!

Life on the Space Station

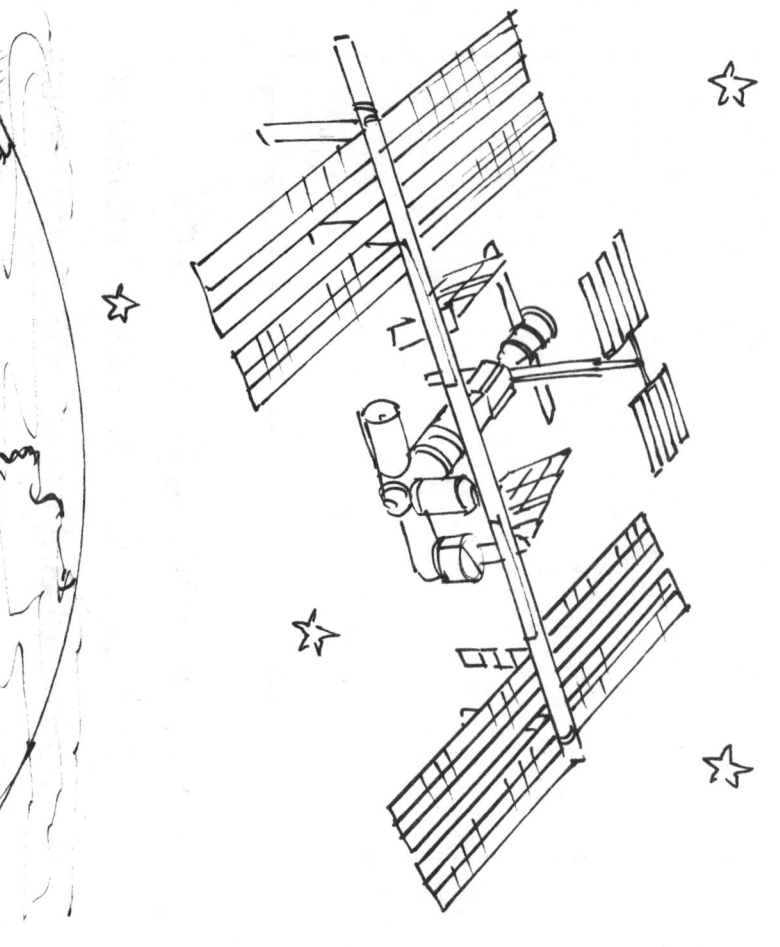

by _____

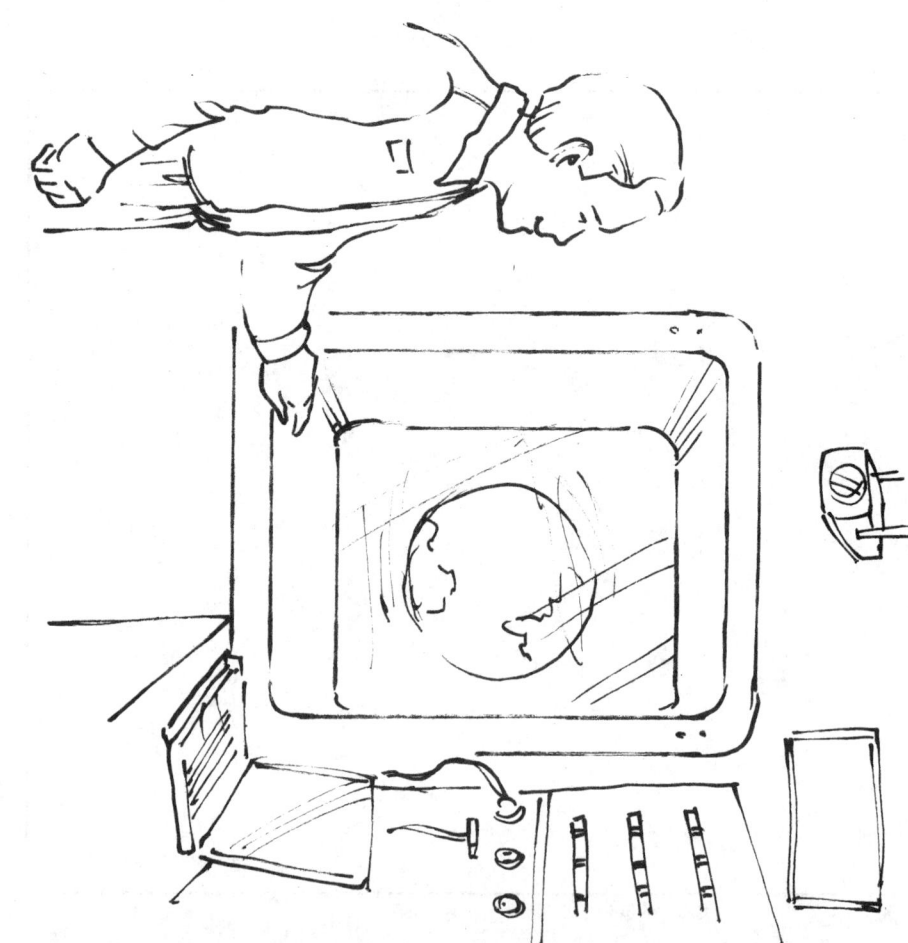

Far out in space, a team of astronauts lives and works. Their home is a space station. It circles Earth at 17,000 miles an hour!

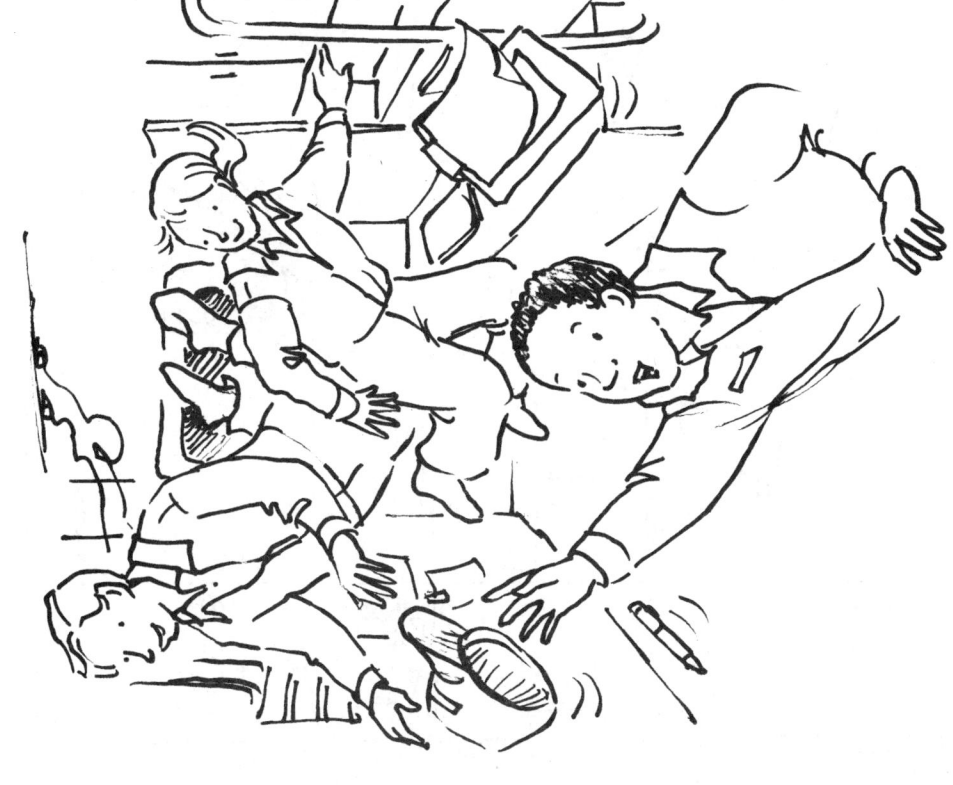

Each day, the three astronauts sleep, eat, and do their work. In space, everything floats—even the people! This makes it hard for astronauts to stay in bed to sleep.

What is life like on a space station? There is not much room at all. Only three astronauts at a time can live there.

At bedtime, the astronauts strap themselves into sleeping bags. The bags hang from the walls! The astronauts say it feels comfortable to sleep this way.

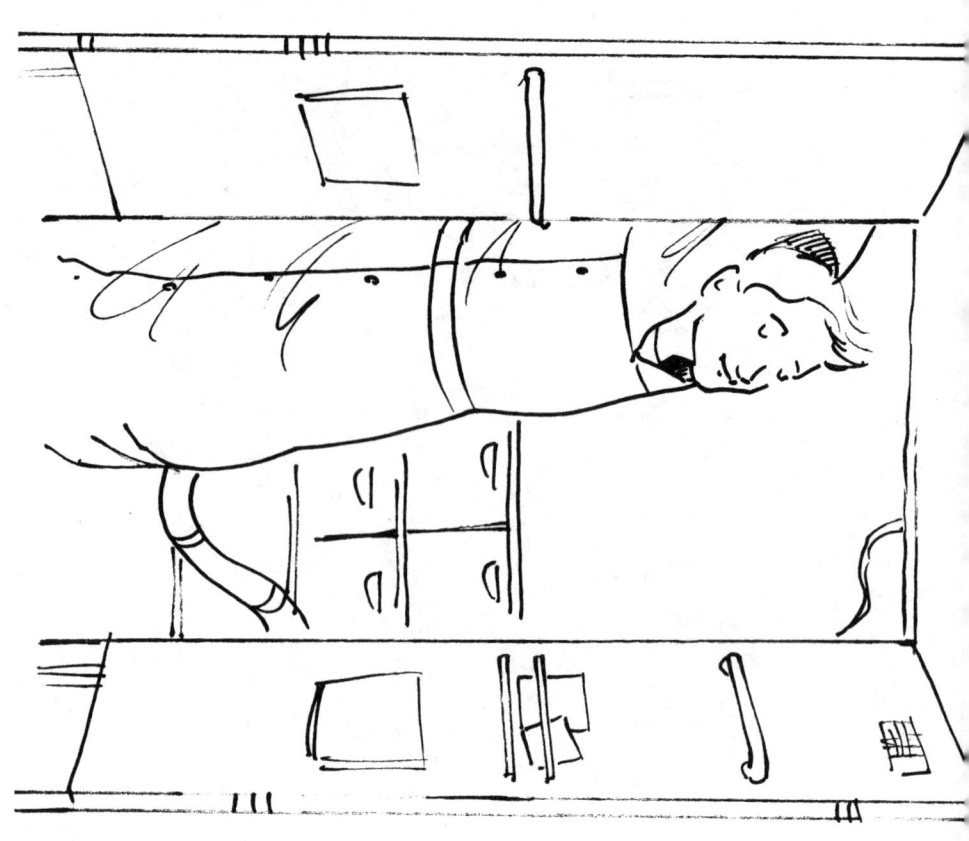

After a good sleep, it's time to eat. Space food comes in cans and special bags. The astronauts add water or heat the bags to prepare their meals.

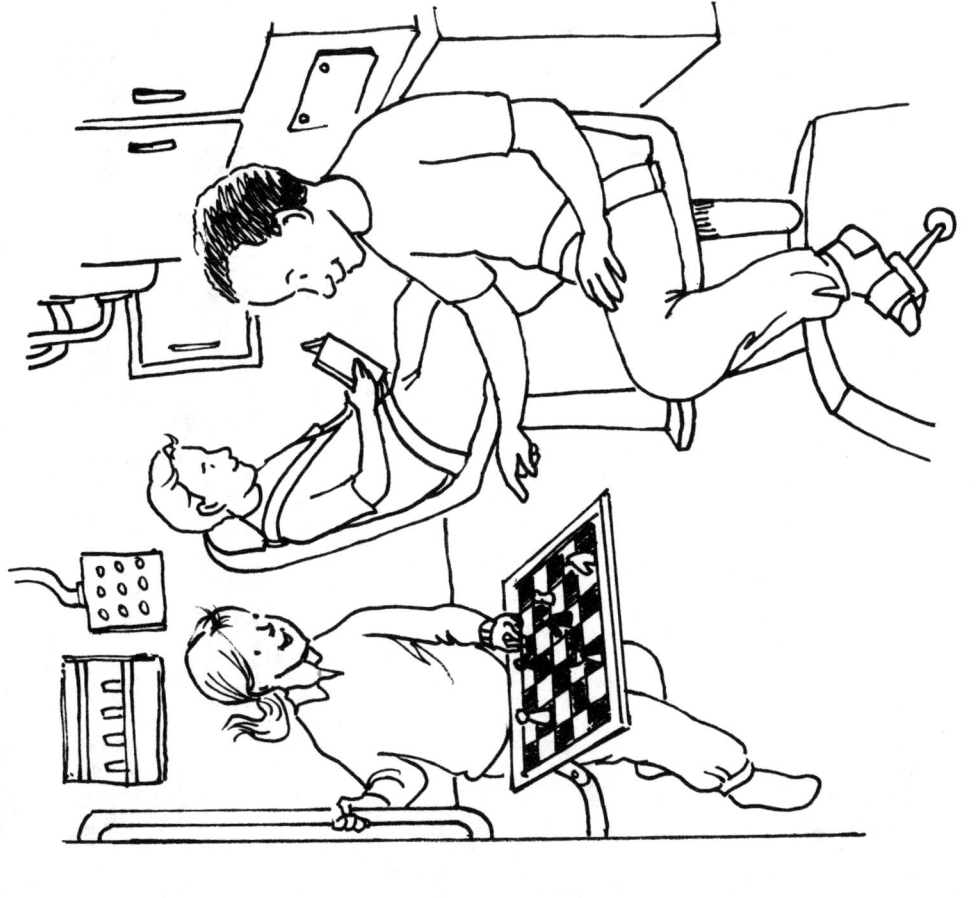

Finally, their work is done. Now the astronauts take time to play and relax. They read, watch movies, and use a computer. They exercise to keep their bodies in shape.

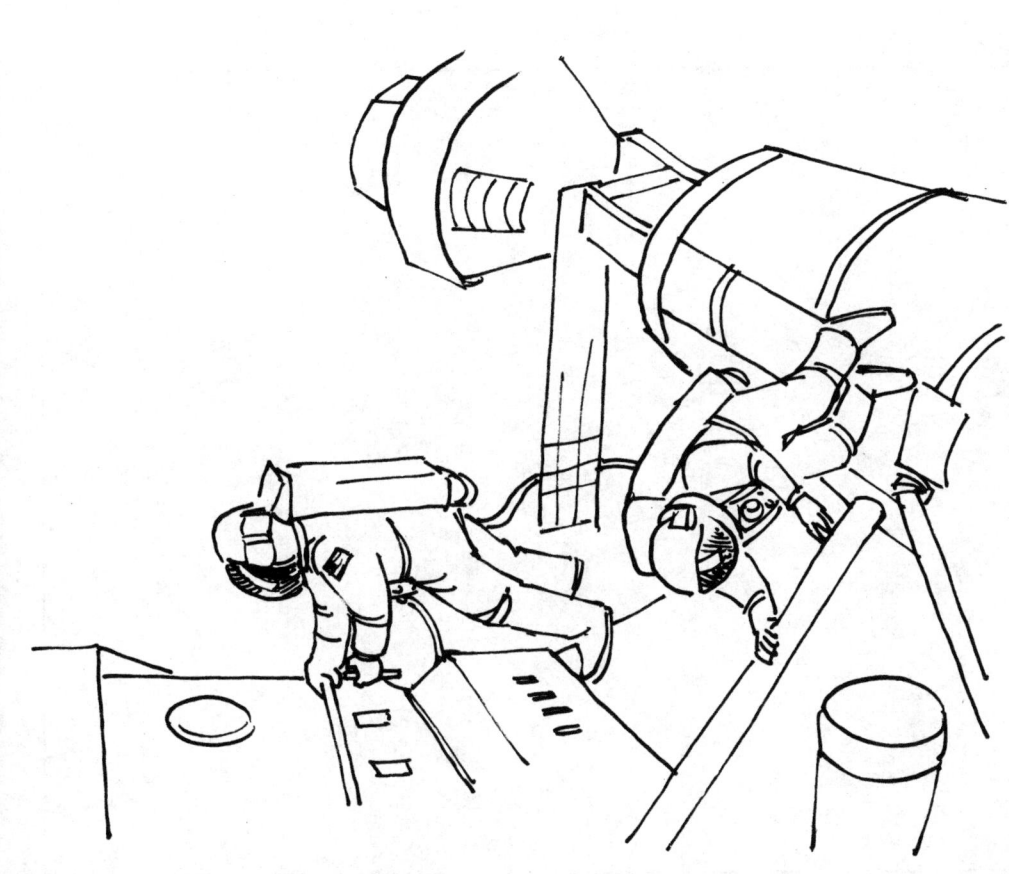

Then the astronauts start their work. They do experiments and walk in space. They add new parts to the space station and make repairs.

Nicole Makes the Team

by _____

At the bus stop one morning, Nicole saw a sign. "Softball tryouts today," it said. "Come and join our team."

As she got on the bus, Nicole thought, "I've never played softball. I can't try out for a team if I've never even played. I'll just go and watch."

After school, Nicole walked to the park where the tryouts were being held. She saw lots of kids batting and catching. A girl named Erin waved at her.

"Hi!" called Erin. "Want to play?"

"I don't know how," said Nicole.

Erin gave Nicole her softball glove. "Put this on," she said. "I'll show you what to do."

At first, Erin threw some balls for Nicole to catch. She caught almost every one! She also tried batting and throwing the ball. "I might be good at softball," Nicole said. "Maybe I will try out."

"SMACK!" Nicole hit the ball. It soared through the air. "Nice hit!" yelled Erin. "Nice hit!" said Nicole to herself.

"Wow," said Nicole to herself.

"I'm going to play softball after all!"

Soon, it was time for tryouts to start. Nicole took her place in line. At last, it was her turn! She caught four balls and threw two to home plate. Then Nicole stepped up to bat.

Growing Up in a Pond

by _____

Glue text box here.

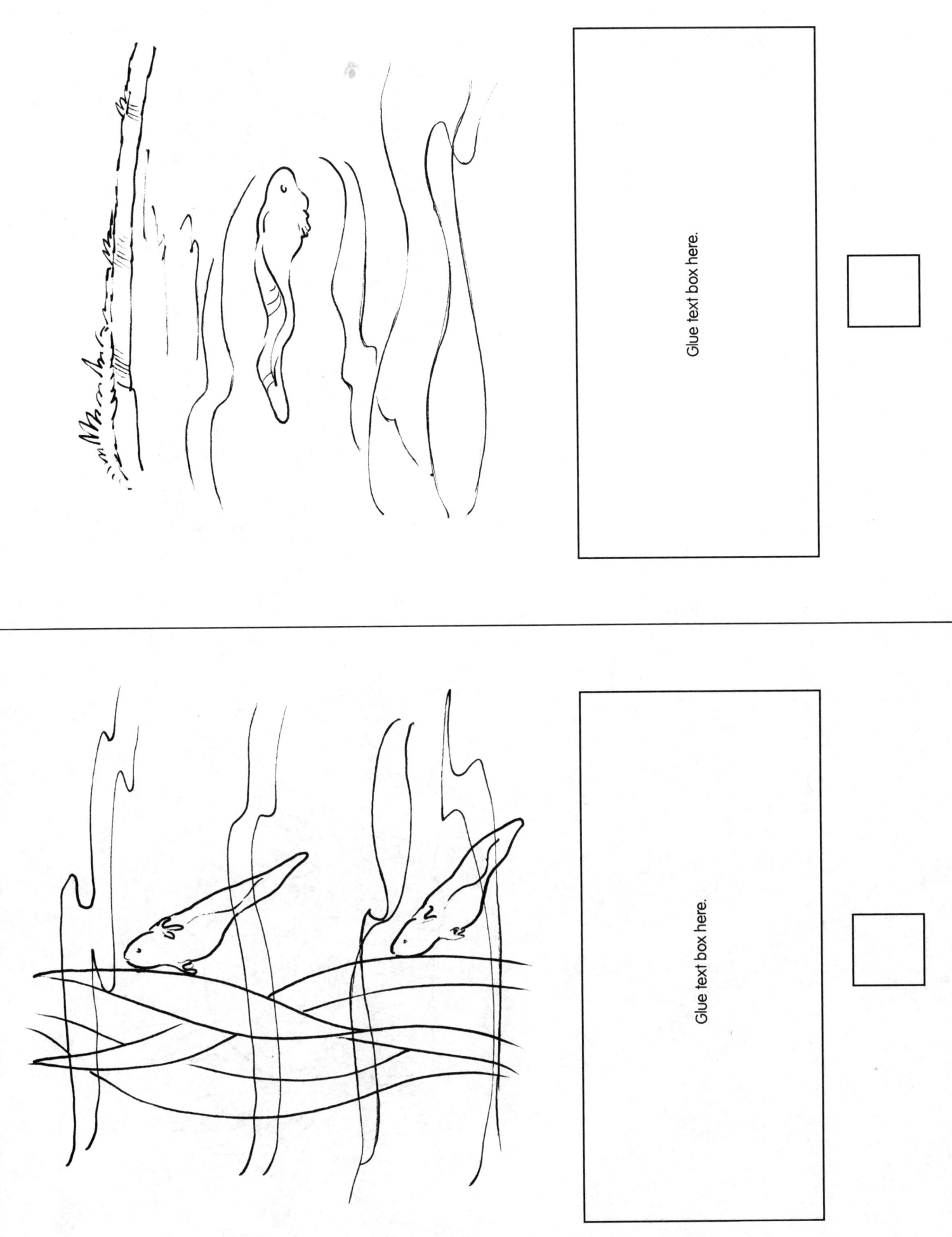

Glue text box here.

Glue text box here.

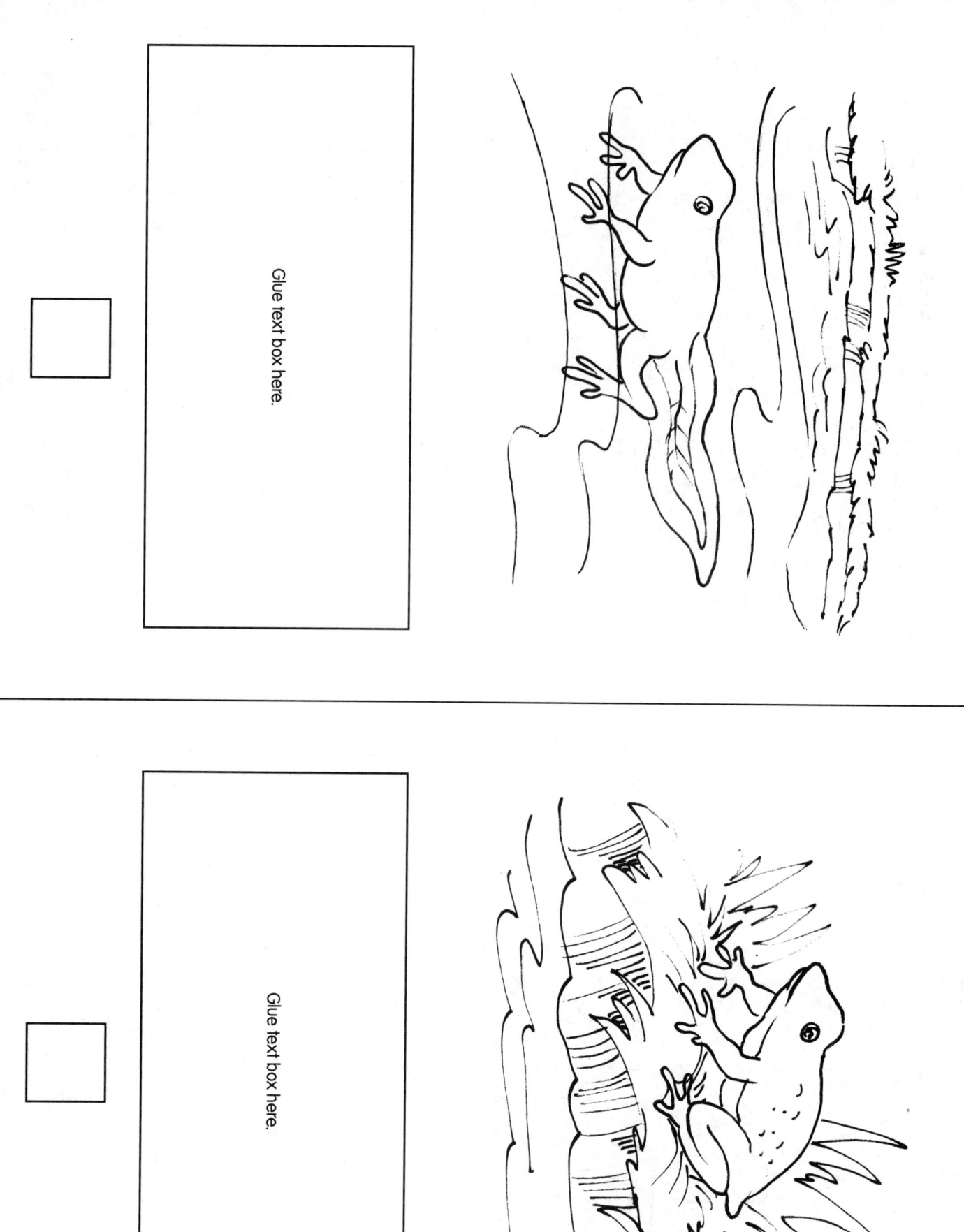

Glue text box here.

Glue text box here.

Glue text box here.

Glue text box here.

**Growing Up
in a Pond**
Text Boxes

As the tadpole grows, its head gets larger and its body gets longer. The back legs, then the front legs, appear. It looks like a tiny frog with a long tail. The tadpole is now a froglet.

The froglet is nearly grown up. It hops on land and swims in the water. Its tail is nearly gone. It uses its long, sticky tongue to catch flies and other bugs.

About seven days later, the tadpole lets go of the grass. It wiggles and swims about like a fish. It eats very tiny plants underwater and uses its gills to breathe.

The froglet's legs grow out. Its tail gets shorter. The gills close up, and it uses lungs to breathe air. Now the froglet can leave the water.

Growing Up in a Pond
Text Boxes

At last, the tail disappears. Skin covers the place where the tail once grew. The froglet is no longer a baby. It has turned into a grown-up frog!

Tadpoles are baby frogs. They hatch from tiny eggs. Grown-up frogs lay many eggs at one time. The eggs stick together. They look like jelly floating on the water.

After about ten days, tadpoles hatch out of the eggs. Each tadpole has gills, a mouth, and a long tail. The tadpole sticks to pond grass at first.

The Magic Bar of Soap

by _____

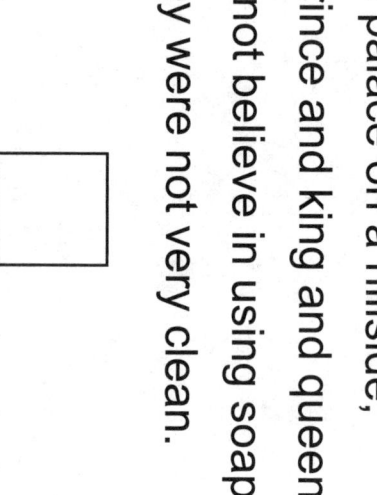

In a palace on a hillside,
a prince and king and queen
did not believe in using soap.
They were not very clean.

☐

They'd cough into their sticky hands,
and there the germs would stay.
And so the king and queen and prince
were sick most every day.

Their royal hands and faces
felt sticky all the time.
And everything their fingers touched
turned black with dirt and grime.

Then something changed their habits.
A guest stayed overnight.
Her hands and face were squeaky clean.
Her clothes were clean and bright.

She brought with her a bar of soap.
"What is it?" asked the three.
"It's magic," said the visitor.
"Add water, and you'll see."

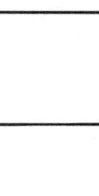

He ordered soap for everyone.

And from that moment on,

they all stayed clean and healthy.

The dirt and germs were gone!

The king stood at the royal sink

and turned the water on.

He rubbed the soap between his hands.

"The dirt!" he cried. "It's gone!"

Growing Sunflowers

by _____

How do you get sunflower seeds to grow into tall plants? Just follow these steps.

To get the seeds ready for planting, fold a paper towel in half. Spray it with water so it is damp but not very wet. Lay a few seeds out across the towel.

First, buy sunflower seeds at a store. Will you grow them in a pot or a garden? Choose the kind of seeds that will grow best where you want to plant them.

Next, lay another damp, folded towel on top of the seeds. Peek at the seeds every day. Check that they stay damp but are not soaked. Seeds will not grow if they are too wet.

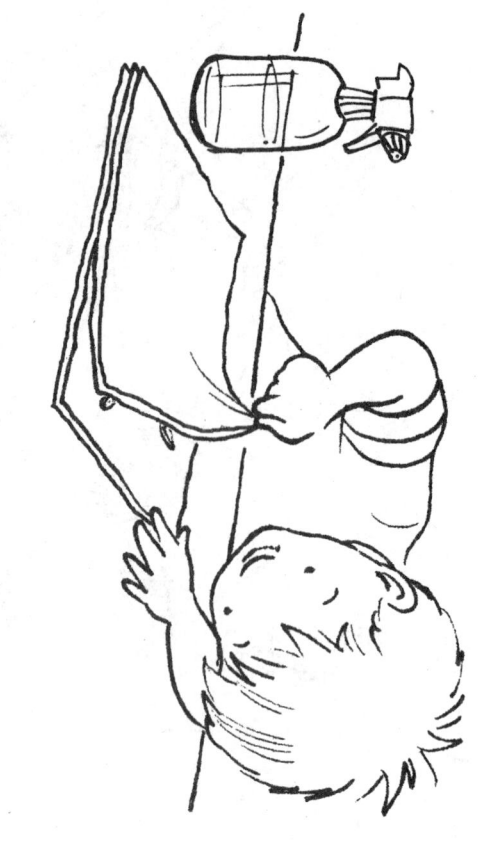

After one or two weeks, the seeds should start to sprout. The first ones to grow are often the strongest. Choose the strongest sprouts to plant.

Put your plants in a sunny place. Sunflowers need lots of sunshine to grow. Also, be sure to keep the soil wet. Before long, you'll have bright, healthy sunflowers!

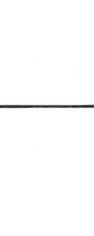

Plant the sprouts one inch apart in soil. Use your finger to make a hole about an inch deep for each sprout. Then cover the roots with soil. Add water until the soil is completely wet.

Happy Birthday, America!

by _____

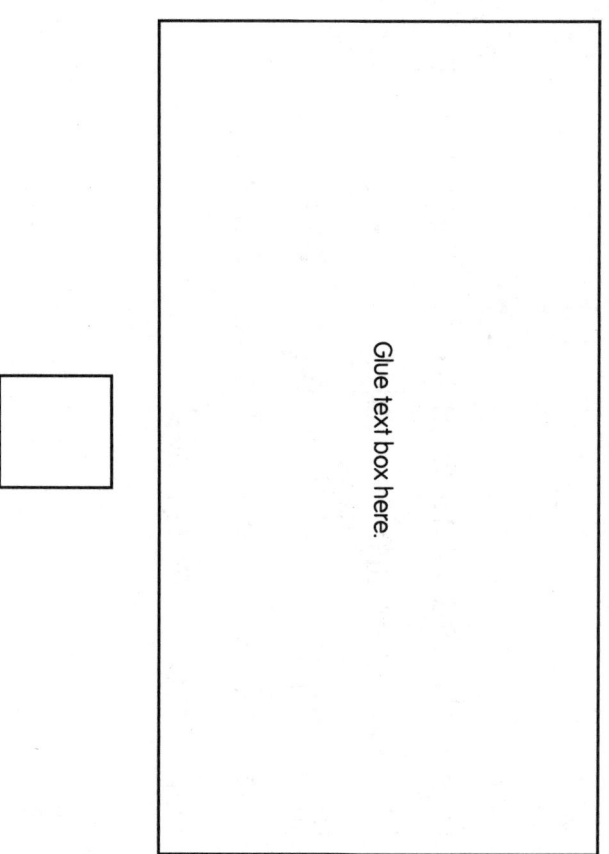

Glue text box here.

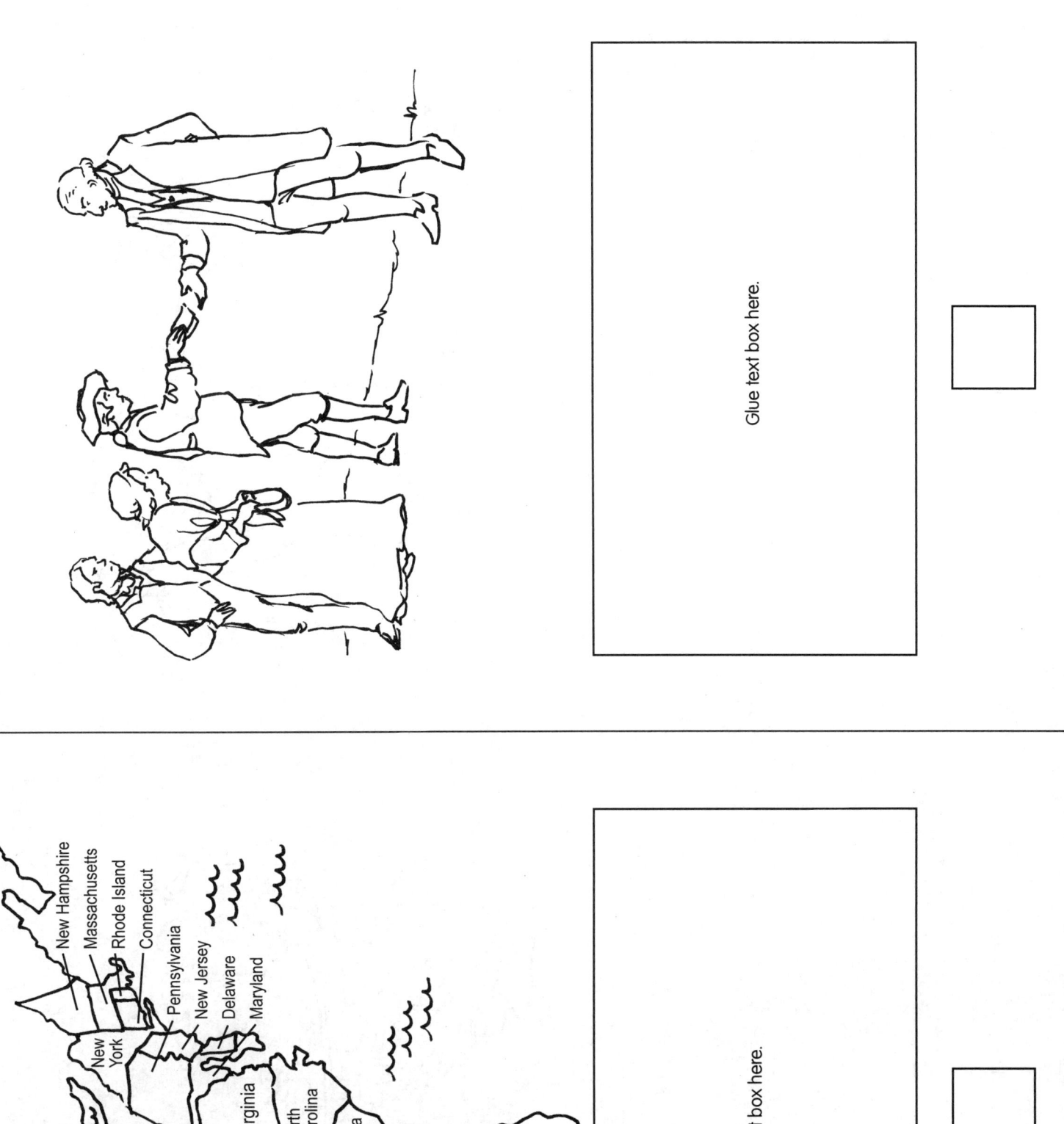

New Hampshire
Massachusetts
Rhode Island
Connecticut
Pennsylvania
New York
New Jersey
Delaware
Maryland
Virginia
North Carolina
South Carolina
Georgia

Glue text box here.

Glue text box here.

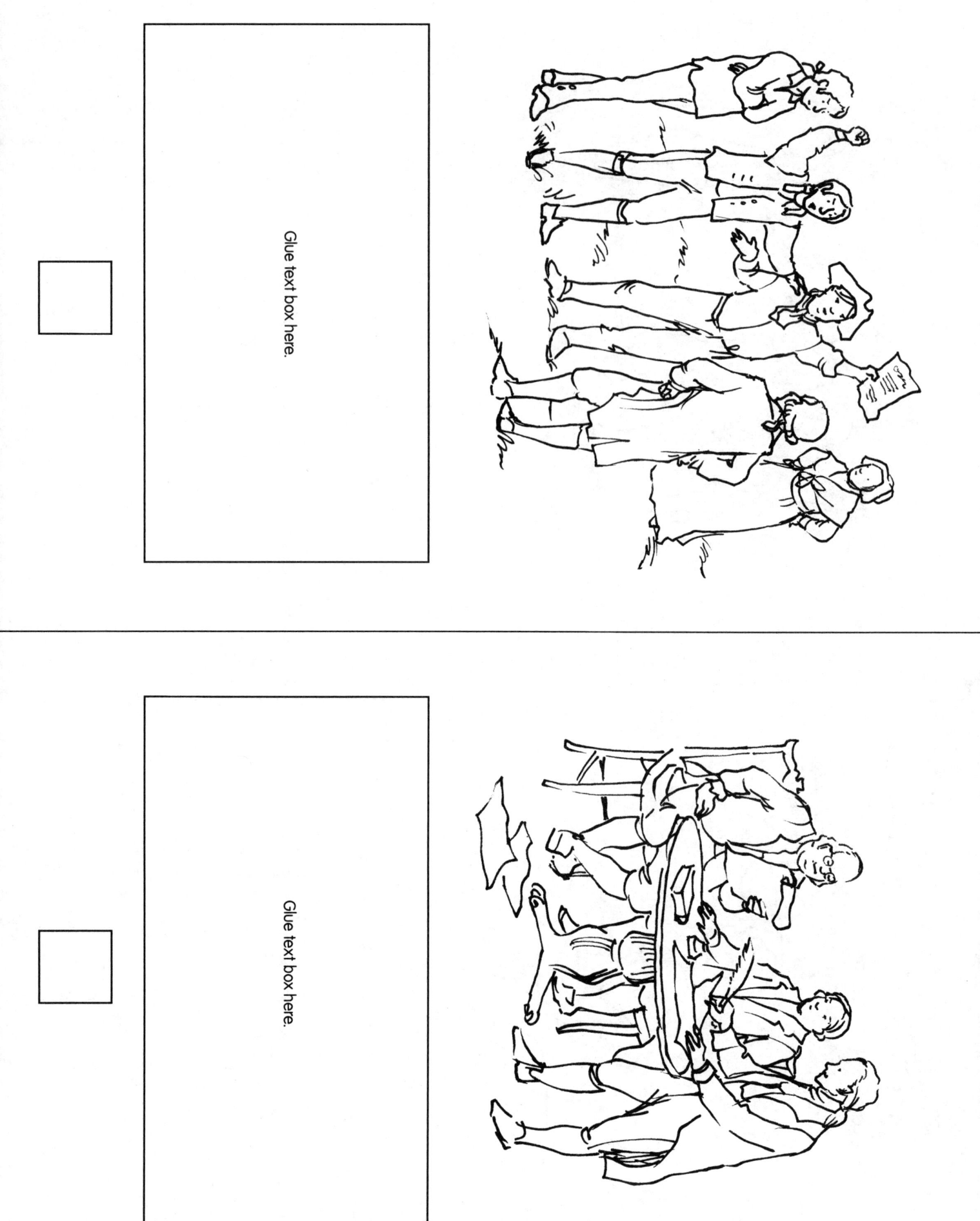

Glue text box here.

Glue text box here.

Glue text box here.

Glue text box here.

Happy Birthday, America!
Text Boxes

Our nation was born in the year 1776. Until then, America was not a country. It was a group of 13 colonies that was owned by a country named England.

How did they break free? First, some American leaders wrote a letter to the king. It said that the colonies did not want to belong to England anymore. The leaders signed the letter on July 4, 1776.

On July Fourth, flags wave across the United States. People hold picnics and watch parades. Fireworks light the skies. Why? July Fourth is our nation's birthday!

America won the war, and England gave up the colonies. Now, each July Fourth, we celebrate America's birthday and the letter that set our country free—the Declaration of Independence!

People who lived in the colonies had to follow England's rules. They had to pay money to England. The King of England sent rulers who made them pay more and more money.

Then a copy of the letter was sent to all 13 colonies. Leaders in each colony read the letter to the people. Most agreed with what it said. Soon, England went to war with America.

The people called England's rules unfair. They said that the king wanted too much money. The colonies wanted to break free from England and become their own country.

Make Your Own Smoothie

by _____

What's yummy, smooth, and totally cool? A fruit smoothie!

A smoothie can be tasty, healthful, and fun to make. For this frozen drink, you'll need juice, fruit, and ice.

First, decide what kind of juice you want to use. Do you like apple, orange, or grape juice? How about mango or cranberry? Pour two cups of juice into the blender.

You'll also need a knife to chop up fruit and a blender to mix the ingredients. Ask a grown-up to help you use these things.

Next, choose a fruit. Are you a banana fan? How do you feel about peaches or watermelon? Peel the fruit and chop it up. You'll need a cup of fruit for your smoothie.

Put the fruit in the blender with the juice. Then add one cup of ice. Put the lid on the blender and turn it on. Let the blender run for one minute.

Now, pour the smoothie into a cup and enjoy your frozen drink. The next time you make a smoothie, you can try a different kind. You can even make smoothies for your friends and family!

After you turn off the blender, lift the lid and peek inside. Is your smoothie thick or thin? If you want it thicker, add some more ice and run the blender again.

Answer Key

School Days Long Ago (pages 9–12)

Make a Friendly Pumpkin (pages 13–16)

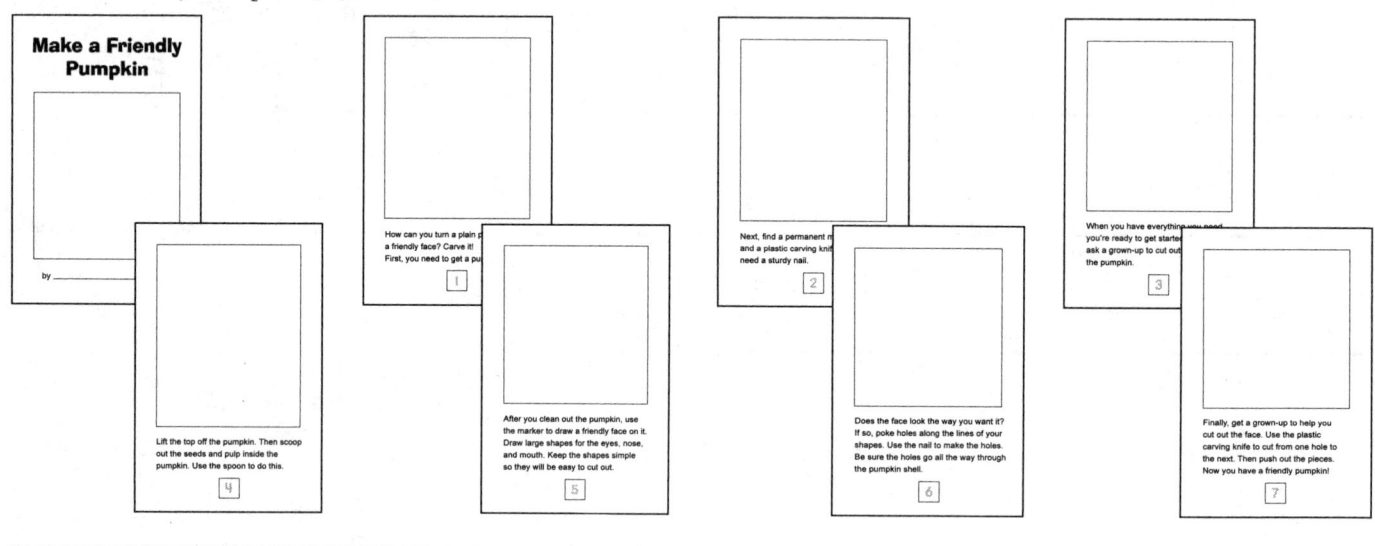

Fire Safety Field Trip (pages 17–22)

Sequencing Practice Mini-Books, Grades 2–3 © 2010 by Kathleen M. Hollenbeck, Scholastic Teaching Resources

Hurrah for Thanksgiving! (pages 23–26)

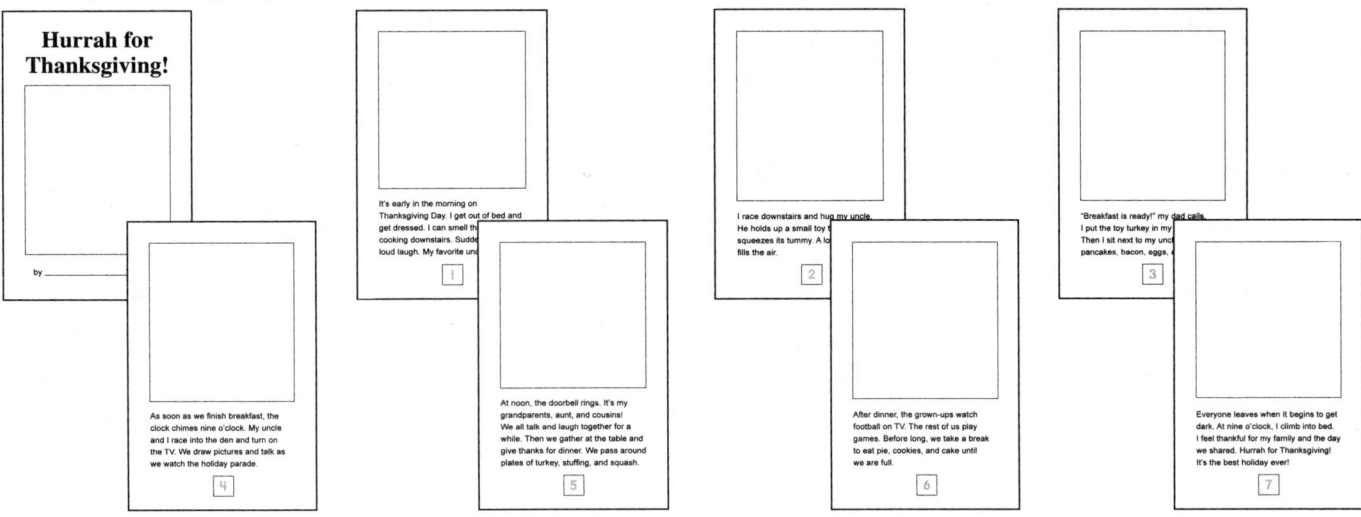

Hurrah for Thanksgiving!

by _____

It's early in the morning on Thanksgiving Day. I get out of bed and get dressed. I can smell th[e] cooking downstairs. Sudde[nly] loud laugh. My favorite unc[le]

1

I race downstairs and hug my uncle. He holds up a small toy [turkey and] squeezes its tummy. A lo[ud gobble] fills the air.

2

"Breakfast is ready!" my dad calls. I put the toy turkey in my [pocket.] Then I sit next to my uncl[e. We eat] pancakes, bacon, eggs, [and more.]

3

As soon as we finish breakfast, the clock chimes nine o'clock. My uncle and I race into the den and turn on the TV. We draw pictures and talk as we watch the holiday parade.

4

At noon, the doorbell rings. It's my grandparents, aunt, and cousins! We all talk and laugh together for a while. Then we gather at the table and give thanks for dinner. We pass around plates of turkey, stuffing, and squash.

5

After dinner, the grown-ups watch football on TV. The rest of us play games. Before long, we take a break to eat pie, cookies, and cake until we are full.

6

Everyone leaves when it begins to get dark. At nine o'clock, I climb into bed. I feel thankful for my family and the day we shared. Hurrah for Thanksgiving! It's the best holiday ever!

7

America's First Woman Doctor (pages 27–30)

America's First Woman Doctor

by _____

Elizabeth Blackwell wanted to be a doctor. She needed to go to school to become one. At that time, [few people] were doctors. Most school[s would not] let a woman in.

1

After many tries, Elizabeth found a school that would let her [in.] People made fun of Eliza[beth. They did] not think women could b[e doctors.]

2

In school, Elizabeth studied hard. She did well on her tests. She even finished at the top of her [class.] Elizabeth was the very fi[rst woman in] America to become a do[ctor.]

3

After graduating, Dr. Elizabeth Blackwell went to other countries to study and work. When she came back to America, no hospital would hire her. But Elizabeth had an idea! She bought a house and used it as a doctor's office!

4

Dr. Blackwell worked from her house for years. Then she opened a hospital for women and children. She also trained others to become nurses.

5

Training nurses gave Dr. Blackwell another idea. She could start a school of her own! Dr. Blackwell began a medical college. Her college was for women who wanted to become doctors.

6

All of her life, Dr. Elizabeth Blackwell helped and served others. She worked hard and led the way for other women to become doctors. Dr. Blackwell made life better for women in America and all over the world.

7

How to Build a Snow Person (pages 31–34)

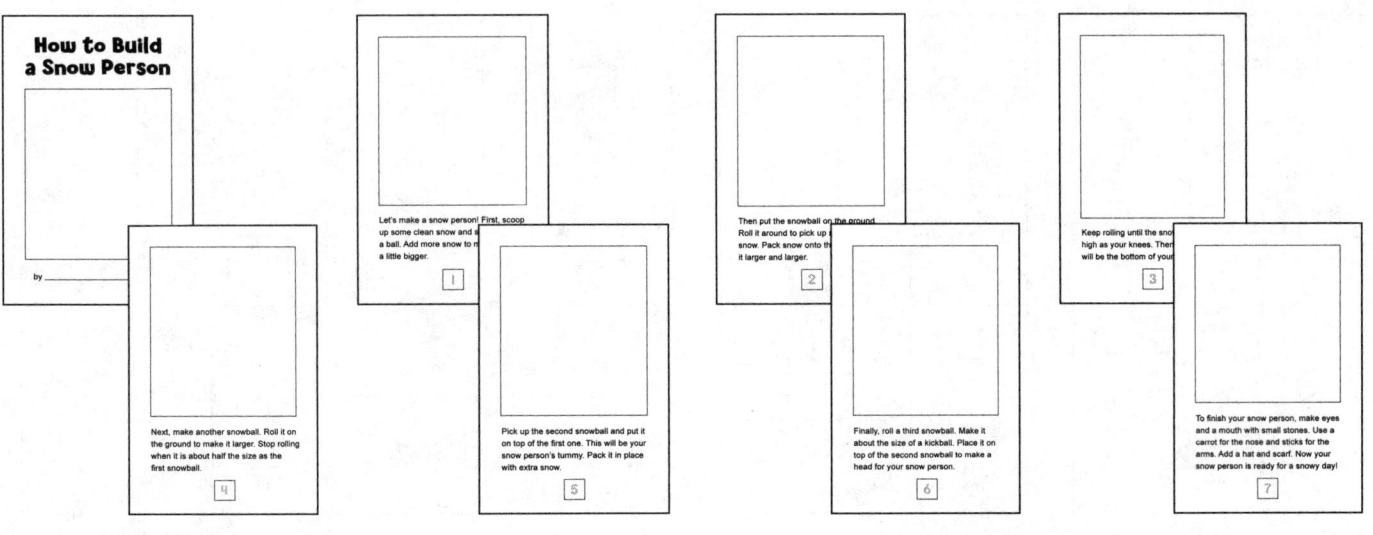

How to Build a Snow Person

by _____

Let's make a snow person! First, scoop up some clean snow and s[hape it into] a ball. Add more snow to m[ake] a little bigger.

1

Then put the snowball on the ground. Roll it around to pick up [more] snow. Pack snow onto th[e ball to make] it larger and larger.

2

Keep rolling until the sno[wball is as] high as your knees. Ther[e it] will be the bottom of your [snow person.]

3

Next, make another snowball. Roll it on the ground to make it larger. Stop rolling when it is about half the size as the first snowball.

4

Pick up the second snowball and put it on top of the first one. This will be your snow person's tummy. Pack it in place with extra snow.

5

Finally, roll a third snowball. Make it about the size of a kickball. Place it on top of the second snowball to make a head for your snow person.

6

To finish your snow person, make eyes and a mouth with small stones. Use a carrot for the nose and sticks for the arms. Add a hat and scarf. Now your snow person is ready for a snowy day!

7

Answer Key

Crocodile Smile (pages 35–39)

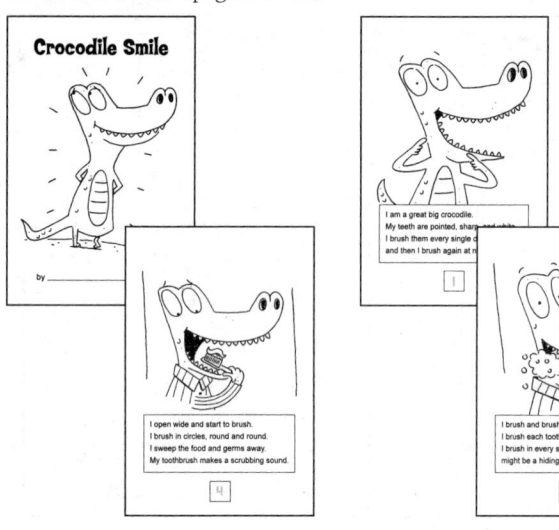

Crocodile Smile

by _____

I am a great big crocodile.
My teeth are pointed, sharp, and white.
I brush them every single [day]
and then I brush again at n[ight].
`1`

To start, I turn the water on
and hold my toothbrush un[der it].
I like to get it nice and wet
so it will slide across my t[eeth].
`2`

Once this is done, I look around
until I find my own toothpa[ste].
I squeeze a little on my br[ush].
I really like the minty taste[.]
`3`

I open wide and start to brush.
I brush in circles, round and round.
I sweep the food and germs away.
My toothbrush makes a scrubbing sound.
`4`

I brush and brush, bottom and top.
I brush each tooth in front and back.
I brush in every spot I think
might be a hiding place for plaque.
`5`

When I am done, my mouth is full.
I spit the foam into the sink.
I turn the water on again
to rinse my brush and get a drink.
`6`

I've brushed my teeth and now I know
I've taken good care of my smile.
My teeth feel clean. My job is done.
I am a happy crocodile.
`7`

Gus Groundhog's Surprise (pages 40–43)

Gus Groundhog's Surprise

by _____

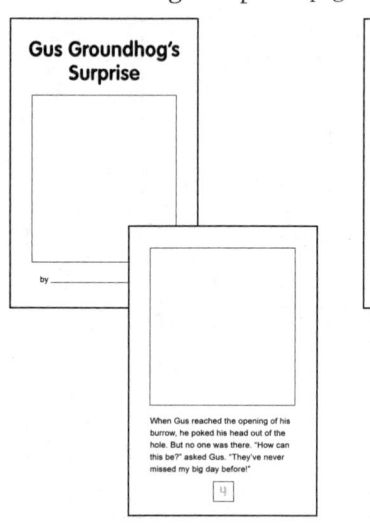

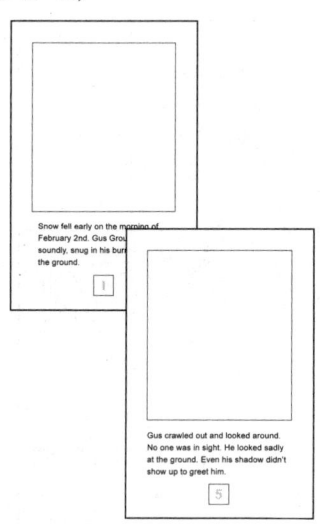

Snow fell early on the morning of
February 2nd. Gus Grou[ndhog slept]
soundly, snug in his burr[ow under]
the ground.
`1`

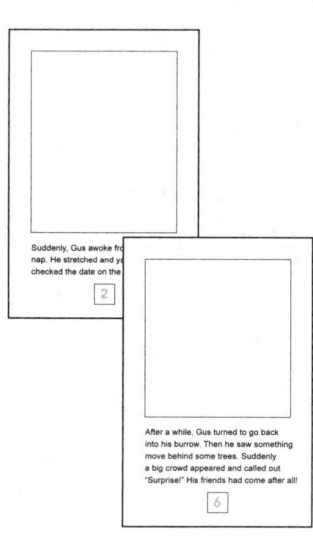

Suddenly, Gus awoke fro[m his]
nap. He stretched and ya[wned. He]
checked the date on the [calendar.]
`2`

"It's Groundhog Day!" he said.
"My friends must be waiting for me."
Gus hurried through his burrow.
He thought about the c[rowd that]
would greet him. How t[hey would]
cheer when they saw h[im!]
`3`

When Gus reached the opening of his
burrow, he poked his head out of the
hole. But no one was there. "How can
this be?" asked Gus. "They've never
missed my big day before!"
`4`

Gus crawled out and looked around.
No one was in sight. He looked sadly
at the ground. Even his shadow didn't
show up to greet him.
`5`

After a while, Gus turned to go back
into his burrow. Then he saw something
move behind some trees. Suddenly
a big crowd appeared and called out
"Surprise!" His friends had come after all!
`6`

"Happy Groundhog Day!" said his
friends. Gus smiled and said, "I knew you
would come! But my shadow didn't show
up. Do you know what that means?"
"Hurray!" they all cheered. "Spring will
be early this year!"
`7`

Life on the Space Station (pages 44–47)

Life on the Space Station

by _____

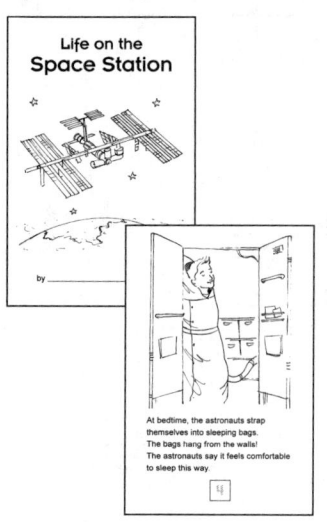

Far out in space, a team of
astronauts lives and works.
Their home is a spac[e station.]
It circles Earth at 17,0[00 miles]
an hour!
`1`

What is life like on a space station?
There is not much roo[m to live.]
Only three astronauts a[t a time]
can live there.
`2`

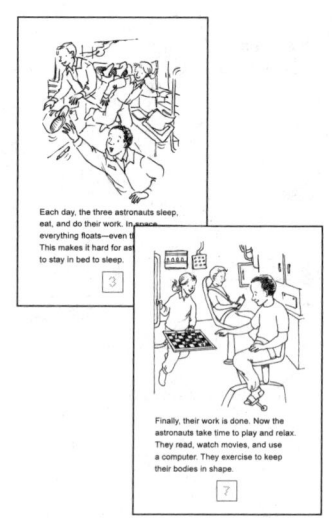

Each day, the three astronauts sleep,
eat, and do their work. In space,
everything floats—even t[he people!]
This makes it hard for ast[ronauts]
to stay in bed to sleep.
`3`

At bedtime, the astronauts strap
themselves into sleeping bags.
The bags hang from the walls!
The astronauts say it feels comfortable
to sleep this way.
`4`

After a good sleep, it's time to eat.
Space food comes in cans and
special bags. The astronauts add
water or heat the bags to prepare
their meals.
`5`

Then the astronauts start their work.
They do experiments and walk in space.
They add new parts to the space station
and make repairs.
`6`

Finally, their work is done. Now the
astronauts take time to play and relax.
They read, watch movies, and use
a computer. They exercise to keep
their bodies in shape.
`7`

Sequencing Practice Mini-Books, Grades 2–3 © 2010 by Kathleen M. Hollenbeck, Scholastic Teaching Resources

Nicole Makes the Team (pages 48–51)

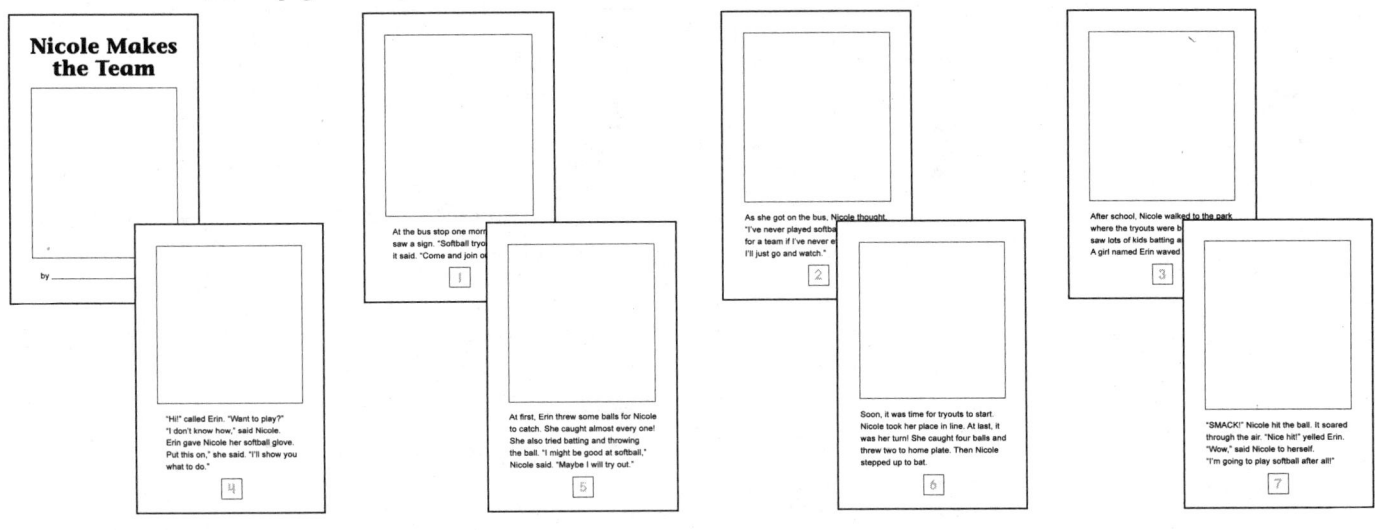

Nicole Makes the Team

by _____

At the bus stop one morn... saw a sign. "Softball tryo... it said. "Come and join o...

1

As she got on the bus, Nicole thought, "I've never played softba... for a team if I've never e... I'll just go and watch."

2

After school, Nicole walked to the park where the tryouts were b... saw lots of kids batting a... A girl named Erin waved...

3

"Hi!" called Erin. "Want to play?"
"I don't know how," said Nicole.
Erin gave Nicole her softball glove.
Put this on," she said. "I'll show you what to do."

4

At first, Erin threw some balls for Nicole to catch. She caught almost every one! She also tried batting and throwing the ball. "I might be good at softball," Nicole said. "Maybe I will try out."

5

Soon, it was time for tryouts to start. Nicole took her place in line. At last, it was her turn! She caught four balls and threw two to home plate. Then Nicole stepped up to bat.

6

"SMACK!" Nicole hit the ball. It soared through the air. "Nice hit!" yelled Erin.
"Wow," said Nicole to herself.
"I'm going to play softball after all!"

7

Growing Up in a Pond (pages 52–57)

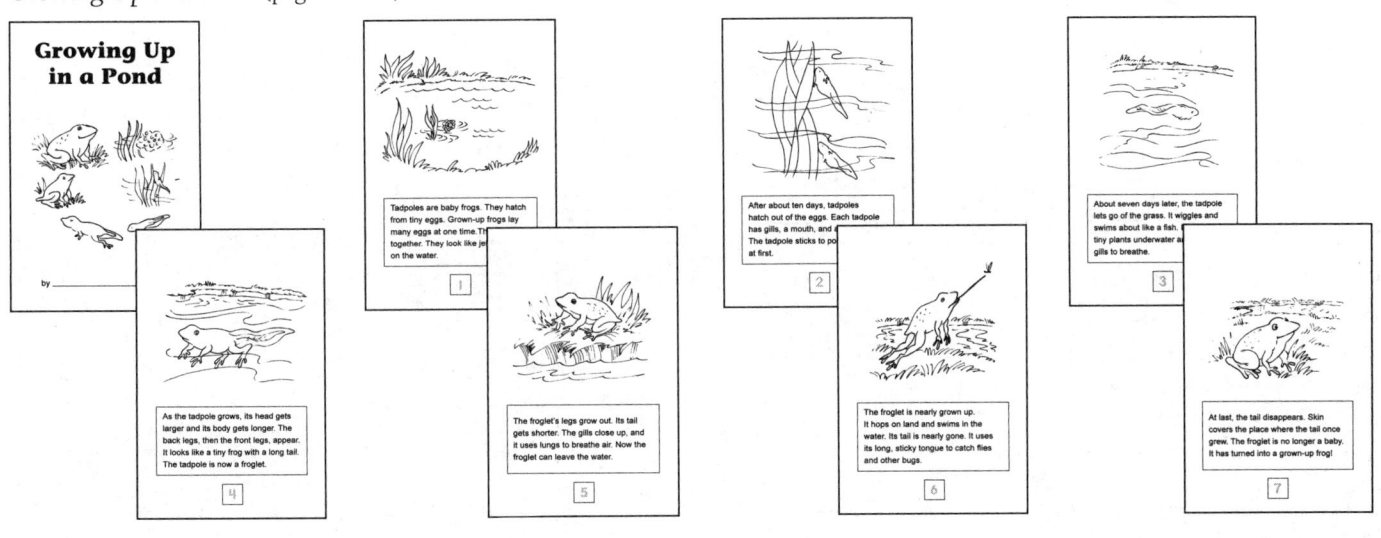

Growing Up in a Pond

by _____

Tadpoles are baby frogs. They hatch from tiny eggs. Grown-up frogs lay many eggs at one time. Th... together. They look like je... on the water.

1

After about ten days, tadpoles hatch out of the eggs. Each tadpole has gills, a mouth, and a... The tadpole sticks to po... at first.

2

About seven days later, the tadpole lets go of the grass. It wiggles and swims about like a fish. It... tiny plants underwater a... gills to breathe.

3

As the tadpole grows, its head gets larger and its body gets longer. The back legs, then the front legs, appear. It looks like a tiny frog with a long tail. The tadpole is now a froglet.

4

The froglet's legs grow out. Its tail gets shorter. The gills close up, and it uses lungs to breathe air. Now the froglet can leave the water.

5

The froglet is nearly grown up.
It hops on land and swims in the water. Its tail is nearly gone. It uses its long, sticky tongue to catch flies and other bugs.

6

At last, the tail disappears. Skin covers the place where the tail once grew. The froglet is no longer a baby. It has turned into a grown-up frog!

7

The Magic Bar of Soap (pages 58–61)

The Magic Bar of Soap

by _____

In a palace on a hillside a prince and king and did not believe in usin... They were not very c...

1

Their royal hands and faces felt sticky all the time.
And everything their fi... turned black with dirt a...

2

They'd cough into their sticky hands and there the germs wou...
And so the king and quee... were sick most every day...

3

Then something changed their habits.
A guest stayed overnight.
Her hands and face were squeaky clean.
Her clothes were clean and bright.

4

She brought with her a bar of soap.
"What is it?" asked the three.
"It's magic," said the visitor.
"Add water, and you'll see."

5

The king stood at the royal sink and turned the water on.
He rubbed the soap between his hands.
"The dirt!" he cried. "It's gone!"

6

He ordered soap for everyone.
And from that moment on,
they all stayed clean and healthy.
The dirt and germs were gone!

7

Growing Sunflowers (pages 62–65)

Growing Sunflowers

by _____

Next, lay another damp, folded towel on top of the seeds. Peek at the seeds every day. Check that they stay damp but are not soaked. Seeds will not grow if they are too wet.

4

How do you get sunflower seeds to grow into tall plants? Just follow these steps.

1

After one or two weeks, the seeds should start to sprout. The first ones to grow are often the strongest. Choose the strongest sprouts to plant.

5

First, buy sunflower seeds at a store. Will you grow them in a pot? Choose the kind of seeds that grow best where you want to plant.

2

Plant the sprouts one inch apart in soil. Use your finger to make a hole about an inch deep for each sprout. Then cover the roots with soil. Add water until the soil is completely wet.

6

To get the seeds ready for planting, fold a paper towel in half. Add water so it is damp but not soaked. Lay a few seeds out across it.

3

Put your plants in a sunny place. Sunflowers need lots of sunshine to grow. Also, be sure to keep the soil wet. Before long, you'll have bright, healthy sunflowers!

7

Happy Birthday, America! (pages 66–71)

Happy Birthday, America!

by _____

The people called England's rules unfair. They said that the king wanted too much money. The colonies wanted to break free from England and become their own country.

4

On July Fourth, flags wave across the United States. People hold picnics and watch parades. Fireworks light the skies. Why? July Fourth is our nation's birthday!

1

How did they break free? First, some American leaders wrote a letter to the king. It said that the colonies did not want to belong to England anymore. The leaders signed the letter on July 4, 1776.

5

Our nation was born in the year 1776. Until then, America was not a country. It was a group of 13 colonies that was owned by a country named England.

2

Then a copy of the letter was sent to all 13 colonies. Leaders in each colony read the letter to the people. Most agreed with what it said. Soon, England went to war with America.

6

People who lived in the colonies had to follow England's rules. They had to pay money to England. The King of England sent rulers who made them pay more and more money.

3

America won the war, and England gave up the colonies. Now, each July Fourth, we celebrate America's birthday and the letter that set our country free—the Declaration of Independence!

7

Make Your Own Smoothie (pages 72–75)

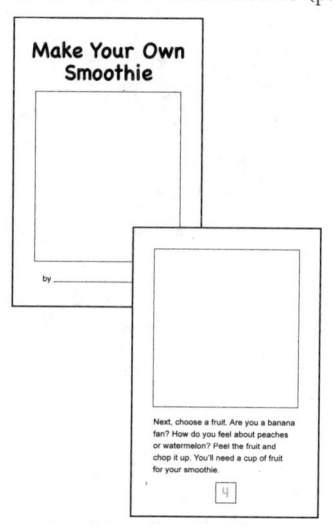

Make Your Own Smoothie

by _____

Next, choose a fruit. Are you a banana fan? How do you feel about peaches or watermelon? Peel the fruit and chop it up. You'll need a cup of fruit for your smoothie.

4

What's yummy, smooth, and totally cool? A fruit smoothie! A smoothie can be tasty, and fun to make. For this you'll need juice, fruit, and

1

Put the fruit in the blender with the juice. Then add one cup of ice. Put the lid on the blender and turn it on. Let the blender run for one minute.

5

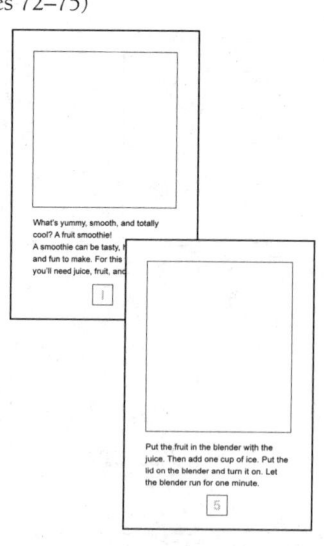

You'll also need a knife and a blender to mix the a grown-up to help you

2

After you turn off the blender, lift the lid and peek inside. Is your smoothie thick or thin? If you want it thicker, add some more ice and run the blender again.

6

First, decide what kind of juice you want to use. Do you like apple, orange, or grape juice? How about cranberry? Pour two cups into the blender.

3

Now, pour the smoothie into a cup and enjoy your frozen drink. The next time you make a smoothie, you can try a different kind. You can even make smoothies for your friends and family!

7

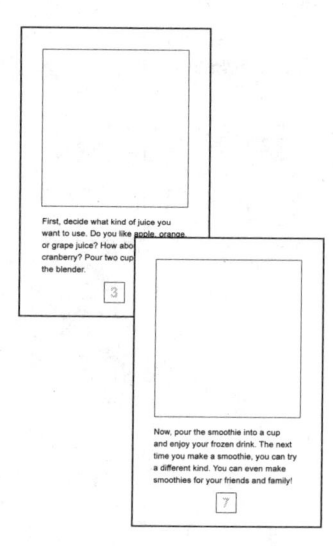

Sequencing Practice Mini-Books, Grades 2–3 © 2010 by Kathleen M. Hollenbeck, Scholastic Teaching Resources